AN APPLE
A DAY

A proverb is one man's wit and all men's wisdom.

LORD JOHN RUSSELL

FROM THE BESTSELLING SERIES

AN APPLE
A DAY

OLD-FASHIONED PROVERBS
AND WHY THEY STILL WORK

CAROLINE TAGGART

Michael O'Mara Books Limited

First published in Great Britain in 2009 by
Michael O'Mara Books Limited
9 Lion Yard
Tremadoc Road
London SW4 7NQ

This edition first published in 2013

A CIP catalogue record for this book is available from the British Library.

Papers used by Michael O'Mara Books Limited are natural, recyclable products made from wood grown in sustainable forests. The manufacturing processes conform to the environmental regulations of the country of origin.

ISBN: 978-1-78243-009-4 in paperback print format
ISBN: 978-1-84317-652-7 in ePub format
ISBN: 978-1-84317-529-2 in Mobipocket format

1 2 3 4 5 6 7 8 9 10

Cover design by Lucy Stephens
Designed and typeset by www.glensaville.com
Printed and bound in Great Britain by CPI Group (UK) Ltd, Croydon, CR0 4YY

www.mombooks.com

Caroline Taggart is the author of a number of best-selling books for Michael O'Mara, including *I Used to Know That* and *My Grammar and I (or should that be 'Me'?)*. Her other books include three *Her Ladyship's Guide to the Queen's English*, *The Book of English Place Names* and *The Book of London Place Names*.

She also appears frequently on radio and TV giving her opinion on such subjects as whether or not there should be an apostrophe in Druids Cross and, if so, where it should go.

Acknowledgements

Many thanks to Toby, Anna, Glen, Ana and everyone else at Michael O'Mara for being such fun to work with. Thanks also to Diana Craig, for toning down my worst excesses but indulging my digressions into Sixties pop. Any remaining excesses are entirely my responsibility.

List of proverbs

Absence makes the heart grow fonder/Out of sight, out of mind

Actions speak louder than words/Fine words butter no parsnips

It takes all sorts to make a world

All that glitters is not gold

All work and no play makes Jack a dull boy

All's fair in love and war/The end justifies the means

All's well that ends well

An apple a day keeps the doctor away

Ask no questions and you'll be told no lies

A bad penny always turns up

A bad workman blames his tools

Beauty is in the eye of the beholder/There's no accounting for taste/Love is blind

Beauty is only skin deep

You've made your bed, so you must lie in it

Beggars can't be choosers

Better late than never

Better the devil you know than the devil you don't

It is better to travel hopefully than to arrive

A bird in the hand is worth two in the bush

Birds of a feather flock together

Once bitten, twice shy

There is none so blind as he who will not see

Blood is thicker than water
You can't get blood out of a stone
Boys will be boys/You're only young once
Brevity is the soul of wit
You can't make bricks without straw
A new broom sweeps clean

You can't have your cake and eat it too
There is always calm after a storm
If the cap fits, wear it
A cat may look at a king
When the cat's away, the mice will play
A change is as good as a rest
Don't change horses in midstream
Plus ça change, plus c'est la même chose
Charity begins at home
The child is father of the man
Children should be seen and not heard
Cleanliness is next to godliness
Every cloud has a silver lining
Cold hands, warm heart
Two's company, three's a crowd
Comparisons are odious
Too many cooks spoil the broth/Many hands make light
    work
Don't count your chickens before they are hatched
In the country of the blind, the one-eyed man is king
The course of true love never did run smooth
Don't cross your bridges before you come to them
You've got to be cruel to be kind

It's no use crying over spilt milk
Curiosity killed the cat

The darkest hour is before the dawn
Desperate situations call for desperate measures
The devil finds work for idle hands
Discretion is the better part of valour
Distance lends enchantment
Do unto others as you would have them do unto you
Give a dog a bad name and hang him
A drowning man will clutch at a straw

The early bird catches the worm
Early to bed, early to rise…
Easier said than done
Easy come, easy go
You've got to eat a peck of dirt before you die
Don't put all your eggs in one basket
An elephant never forgets
An Englishman's home is his castle
Enough is as good as a feast
To err is human, to forgive divine
Every little helps
Everything comes to those who wait
The exception proves the rule
What the eye doesn't see, the heart doesn't grieve over

Familiarity breeds contempt
Fling enough dirt and some will stick
A fool and his money are soon parted

Only fools and horses work
Fools rush in where angels fear to tread
Forewarned is forearmed
A friend in need is a friend indeed

Give a man enough rope and he'll hang himself
You can't serve God and Mammon
God helps those who help themselves
Whom the gods love dies young
What goes around comes around
One good turn deserves another
Good wine needs no bush
The grass is always greener on the other side of the fence

Half a loaf is better than no bread
The hand that rocks the cradle rules the world
Handsome is as handsome does
You might as well be hanged for a sheep as for a lamb
More haste, less speed
Two heads are better than one
Hell hath no fury like a woman scorned
He who hesitates is lost/Better safe than sorry
Home is where the heart is/There's no place like home
Honesty is the best policy
There is honour among thieves
Hope springs eternal in the human breast
You can take a horse to water but you can't make it drink
Hunger is the best sauce

Where ignorance is bliss, 'tis folly to be wise

It's an ill wind that blows no one any good
Imitation is the sincerest form of flattery

Jack of all trades is master of none
If a job's worth doing, it's worth doing well
Never judge a book by its cover

Knowledge is power

It's the last straw that breaks a camel's back
Laugh and the world laughs with you
He who laughs last laughs longest
Laughter is the best medicine
Least said soonest mended
A leopard cannot change his spots
Lightning never strikes twice in the same place
A little learning is a dangerous thing
Little things please little minds
Live and let live
The longest journey begins with a single step
Don't look a gift horse in the mouth
Look before you leap
What you lose on the swings you gain on the roundabouts
Love is blind

Every man has his price
A man is known by the company he keeps
A man's best friend is his dog
One man's meat is another man's poison
Manners makyth man

Marry in haste, repent at leisure
A miss is as good as a mile
Money doesn't grow on trees

Necessity is the mother of invention
Needs must when the devil drives
No news is good news/Bad news travels fast
Noblesse oblige
There's nothing new under the sun
Nothing ventured, nothing gained/Faint heart never won
    fair lady/Fortune favours the brave

You can't make an omelette without breaking eggs

Patience is a virtue
He who pays the piper calls the tune
The pen is mightier than the sword
Take care of the pennies and the pounds will take care of
    themselves
In for a penny, in for a pound
People who live in glass houses shouldn't throw stones
Little pitchers have big ears
Possession is nine points of the law
Practice makes perfect
Prevention is better than cure
Pride goes before a fall
Procrastination is the thief of time/Never put off until
    tomorrow what you can do today
The proof of the pudding is in the eating
A prophet is without honour in his own country

Punctuality is the politeness of kings

You can't fit a quart into a pint pot

It never rains but it pours
Revenge is sweet/Revenge is a dish best served
    (or eaten) cold
The road to hell is paved with good intentions
All roads lead to Rome
A rolling stone gathers no moss
Rome wasn't built in a day
When in Rome, do as the Romans do

What's sauce for the goose is sauce for the gander
The best laid schemes o' mice an' men gang aft a-gley
Seeing is believing
Silence is golden...
You can't make a silk purse out of a sow's ear
Let sleeping dogs lie
There's many a slip 'twixt the cup and the lip
Slow but steady wins the race
There's no smoke without fire
As you sow, so shall you reap
Spare the rod and spoil the child
Sticks and stones may break my bones, but words will never
    hurt me
Still waters run deep
A stitch in time saves nine
Strike while the iron is hot
If at first you don't succeed, try, try again

You must suffer to be beautiful
One swallow doesn't make a summer

You can't take it with you
Talk/speak of the devil and he will appear
You can't teach an old dog new tricks
There's a time and a place for everything
Time flies when you're enjoying yourself
Time is a great healer/Time heals all wounds
Time is money
There's no time like the present
There's many a true word spoken in jest
Truth/fact is stranger than fiction
There's many a good tune played on an old fiddle

United we stand, divided we fall

Variety is the spice of life
Virtue is its own reward

Walls have ears
A watched pot never boils
Where there's a will there's a way
Even a worm will turn
Two wrongs don't make a right

Zeal without knowledge is the sister of folly

AN APPLE
A DAY

Introduction

If, when you picked up this book, you asked yourself, '*Another* dictionary of proverbs? Do we need one?' or 'What exactly is a proverb anyway?', read on. I hope to answer both those questions in the next two pages. If you didn't, please feel free to do what most people do — skip this introduction and get on with the book.

Oh hello. Are you still there? OK, here goes.

First of all, this isn't another dictionary of proverbs (there are plenty of them already, several of which are listed in the Bibliography). I have looked at proverbs not necessarily from the point of view of their origins,[1] as the scholarly books do, but to see if they have any relevance today. Interestingly enough, it turns out that most of them do. The insights that struck a chord with Aesop's readers in Ancient Greece, or Shakespeare's audiences 400 years ago, hold good in a surprising number of cases, and have inspired generations of pop songs to prove it.

Secondly, the short answer to 'What is a proverb?' is 'a piece of wisdom or advice, expressed in a short and memorable way'. A proverb may come from almost anywhere, including the mists of time: if you take just three examples — 'An apple a day keeps the doctor away', 'Look before you leap' and 'Better late than never' — you'll find that they are, respectively, a nineteenth-

---

1 Unless they are — as many are — quotations from *Hamlet*.

century saying that people tried to pretend was a much older piece of folk wisdom; the moral of one of Aesop's fables; and a quotation from the first-century Roman historian Livy. As you flick through this book you'll also find many references to Shakespeare and other poets, and to the Bible. So when does a saying stop being a quotation and attain proverbial status; and at what point does it cease to be a proverb and become a mere cliché? And why do so many of them – such as 'Too many cooks spoil the broth'/ 'Many hands make light work' – contradict each other?

Well, any expression that is overused becomes a cliché, but that doesn't stop it having a grain of truth in it. It is overused precisely because it *does* have a grain of truth in it. To become a proverb, a saying has to have something true or useful to say to pretty well everyone. It can occasionally be taken literally ('Early to bed, early to rise,/Makes a man healthy, wealthy and wise') but is usually meant in a metaphorical sense. Despite everything I have written about violins on p. 175, for example, 'There's many a good tune played on an old fiddle' becomes proverbial only when it has nothing to do with stringed instruments and is expanded into a wider context.

As for the contradictions, I think (and as a result of writing this book I have given it more thought than I would have believed possible six months ago) that the 'Too many cooks'/'Many hands' pairing is not as daft as it at first seems – *see* p. 62. I'm on dodgier ground with 'Look before you leap'/'He who hesitates is lost', but hey, these are proverbs

– we're not going to end up in jail or fall foul of health and safety regulations if we don't obey them. The originators of proverbs lived thousands of years apart. Some of them were bold, some of them were timid. Each individual phrase-maker and soundbite-coiner had his own cultural background, his own world view and moral compass, possibly his own axe to grind. He may not even have believed what he was writing – he may just have thought it sounded good. When Shakespeare wrote, 'Brevity is the soul of wit,' for instance, he was certainly mocking the garrulous character who speaks the line.

So what this boils down to is that, however wise they may sound, you can't live your life by proverbs. (You can't make an omelette without breaking eggs, either, nor can you make a silk purse out of a sow's ear, just in case you were thinking of trying.) Some proverbs are valid, some are not; some will apply to your circumstances and appear to solve your problems; others will just confuse you all the more. So read, enjoy, ponder if you feel like it, glean what you find useful, ignore the rest. And don't worry if you don't reach any firm conclusions: it is, after all, better to travel hopefully than to arrive.

CAROLINE TAGGART, London

Absence *makes the heart grow fonder/Out of sight, out of mind*

OH GOOD GRIEF! – the first entry in the book and it's confusing already. Well, console yourself with the thought that although proverbs are supposed to be pieces of wisdom, they aren't immune to differences of opinion. Think Plato versus Aristotle, or Richard Dawkins versus God.

The earliest-known adherent of the first school of thought was the Roman poet Sextus Propertius (first century BC) who, in his *Elegies*, maintains: 'Always toward absent lovers love's tide stronger flows.' An anonymous English poem, dating from 1602, gave us the contemporary wording, but it wasn't until the nineteenth century that the saying became popular, thanks to a song called 'Isle of Beauty', by Thomas Haynes Bayly (1797–1839). It includes the lines:

Absence makes the heart grow fonder,
Isle of Beauty, fare thee well!

The opposing proverb has roots that go back to at least the thirteenth century, but it was John Heywood's *Workes. A dialogue containing proverbs and epigrams*, dating from 1562, that first set it out in black and white.

Credit for finding a sensible middle ground should perhaps go to a seventeenth-century Frenchman called the Comte de Bussy-Rabutin, who wrote:

Absence is to love what wind is to fire,
It extinguishes the small, it kindles the great.

In the case of 'small' love, therefore, 'Out of sight, out of mind' is likely to win out, while straying into the realms of 'When the cat's away the mice will play' may also be a possibility.

Actions *speak louder than words/Fine words butter no parsnips*

IN OTHER WORDS, never mind the pretty speeches, let's see you do something about it — or, to express it another way, fancy talk won't put food on the table. There are many variations on this theme and they've been around for a long time. The New Testament epistle of James tells us, 'Be ye doers of the word, and not hearers only,' and a prolific medieval poet and monk called John Lydgate wrote (I've updated his spelling, as I have with similar quotations throughout this book), 'Word is but wind; leave word and take the deed.' In *Hamlet*[2] Shakespeare has Ophelia say to her brother Laertes, who has just told her to behave herself while he is away:

Do not, as some ungracious pastors do,
Show me the steep and thorny way to heaven;

---

2   Take note of that name. It'll crop up again.

Whilst like a puff'd and reckless libertine,
Himself the primrose path of dalliance treads.

More recently, in the 1970s the Polish–born mathematician and humanist Jacob Bronowski expressed the same idea as, 'The word can only be grasped by action, not by contemplation... The hand is the cutting edge of the mind.'

In short, almost anyone who is anyone has had something to say about actions speaking louder than words, and sitting here thinking about it won't get those parsnips buttered.

It takes **all** *sorts to make a world*

THIS HAS A rather patronizing tone to it, to my mind, as if the speaker wanted to add, '...unfortunately' or '...but in your case I'd like to make an exception.' For some reason it seems to be a favourite expression in detective fiction: my reference books quote Ruth Rendell and Reginald Hill among the authors who have used it. On the other hand, it was also uttered by Cervantes in his *Don Quixote* – 'In the world there must bee of all sorts' – and Dr Johnson, proving that if nothing else it takes all sorts to make a dictionary of quotations.

All *that glitters is not gold*

MEANING 'DO NOT be dazzled by appearances' or 'A bastard who owns a Porsche is still a bastard', this is a quotation from Shakespeare's *The Merchant of Venice* (although in the original the word was 'glisters'). The Prince of Morocco, a suitor for Portia's hand, has to choose between gold, silver and bronze caskets in the hope of finding her portrait inside; he chooses the gold, finds a scroll with these words written on it and is obliged to give up thoughts of marrying anyone in the immediate future.

But Shakespeare was not the first to suggest that appearances can be deceptive. Many others, before and since, have taken up the theme. Back in the twelfth century, the French theologian Alain de Lille warned, 'Do not hold everything gold that shines like gold,' and in 1553, in *The Relikes of Rome*, Thomas Becon reiterated, 'All is not gold that glisterith.' In 1587, in *Tragical Tales (and other poems)*, George Turberville drily observed, 'All is not gold that glisteringly appear.'

The English poet Thomas Gray, author of the famous 'Elegy Written in a Country Churchyard', also wrote a poem with one of the best titles ever, 'On a Favourite Cat, Drowned in a Tub of Gold Fishes'. In this he warned that:

Not all that tempts your wand'ring eyes
And heedless hearts, is lawful prize;
Nor all that glisters, gold.

The aforementioned Thomas Haynes Bayly (*see* 'Absence makes the heart grow fonder'), in a song called 'Fly Away, Pretty Moth', put it a different way:

Be content with the moon and the stars, pretty moth,
And make use of your wings while you may…
Many things in this world that look bright, pretty moth,
Only dazzle to lead us astray.

Sad but true. Remember the bastard with the Porsche I mentioned earlier?

All work and no play makes Jack a dull boy

A COMMON-SENSE PROVERB warning against workaholism and advocating the importance of 'me time'. Its earliest appearance is thought to have been in James Howell's *Proverbs in English, Italian, French and Spanish*, published in 1659. But of course it's not good to go completely the other way either, as the Anglo-Irish novelist Maria Edgeworth (1767–1849) pointed out in 1825, in *Harry and Lucy Concluded*, when she added a second line to the familiar saying:

All work and no play makes Jack a dull boy,
All play and no work makes Jack a mere toy.

All's *fair in love and war/*
The end justifies the means

THERE AREN'T MANY proverbs that seem to be designed as an excuse for bad behaviour, but these are two of them. *The Oxford Dictionary of Proverbs* quotes this example from a 1963 edition of the *Spectator*: 'All is fair in love and war, and it is important that you sustain your marriage. You must therefore take the following, deceitful steps...'

Isn't that tantalizing? Doesn't it leave you desperate to know more? Sadly, short of traipsing over to the *Spectator* offices to see if they keep back numbers, there is no way of finding out more, so let's move on.

Two early versions of the same idea say that 'an impiety may lawfully be committed in love, which is lawless', and 'love and war are all one... it is lawful to use sleights and stratagems to attain the wished end.'

The parallel between love and war is a tenuous one here, I feel: it would be nice — if perhaps a tad naive — to think that most people going to war believe they have right on their side and therefore any means of defeating the enemy is justified.[3] Whether you can say this when you are in love is quite another matter, and when the

---

3 Hmm. Carpet bombing and indiscriminate shelling of civilian areas? Discuss.

saying is adopted – as it frequently is nowadays – into business practice, it becomes very dodgy indeed.

All's *well that ends well*

THIS IS THE title of a play by Shakespeare with a rather repellent plot that involves a man treating a woman like dirt and getting away with it. Have you noticed how often this happens in Shakespeare's comedies? *The Taming of the Shrew* is a positive hymn to male arrogance, and in *Two Gentlemen of Verona* something close to a rape is forgiven and forgotten in the course of a few lines. The women involved then happily marry these loathsome creatures and expect to live happily ever after. What are they *thinking* of?

As is often the case with Shakespeare, he didn't invent the expression but adopted something from popular speech and helped it achieve proverbial status. The reasoning is still specious, though: see the previous entry for more on similar lines.

An **apple** *a day keeps the doctor away*

A COMMON BRITISH folk saying, this is one of the few proverbs that can be taken at face value: 'apples are good for you' is all it means. The Romans knew this and so did the Anglo-Saxons, who listed the crab apple as one of the nine healing plants given to the world by the god Woden. They probably didn't know, as we now do, that apples contain fibre, antioxidants and sundry vitamins and minerals that help to prevent osteoporosis, heart disease and various forms of cancer. But they did know that they were cooling, cleansing and soothing, whether taken as a natural diuretic or applied externally to inflammations.

An anonymous medieval text called *The Haven of Health* recommended eating an apple to relieve your feelings if you were going to bed alone, while Ayurvedic medicine says that apples cure headaches and promote vitality. So the jury is out on whether or not apples are good for your sex life, but they are certainly good for pretty much everything else.

Ask no questions and you'll be told no lies

THE FIRST RECORDED instance can be found in Oliver Goldsmith's *She Stoops to Conquer* (1773): 'Ask me no questions and I'll tell you no fibs.' In a more general sense, however, the phrase is clearly nonsense. You can sit quietly at home, not asking any questions, watching the news on TV and hear politicians lie to you all the time. But I don't think this proverb is aimed at news-watching adults. It's more likely to be uttered by the sort of people who also include 'Children should be seen and not heard' in their repertoire.

A **bad** penny always turns up

ORIGINATING IN THE eighteenth century, this used to mean that if you found yourself with a counterfeit or foreign coin in your possession and you palmed it off on someone else, and they did the same, and their victim did the same again, the coin would eventually find its way back to you. Not very likely, you might say. A more plausible explanation may be that if you tried to slip a shopkeeper a 'bad', i.e. forged, penny, you wouldn't get away with it; it would be given back to you.

Metaphorically the saying means that a troublemaker always reappears on the scene, or that bad deeds return to haunt the perpetrator.

A **bad** workman blames his tools

THE MEANING OF this is obvious: someone who isn't good at their job puts the blame on their tools and equipment. The truth of this statement has long been recognized and there are numerous variations on the theme, among the earliest being the thirteenth-century French saying, 'A bad workman will never find a good tool.' The seventeenth century brought us: 'A bungler cannot find good tools' and 'Never had ill workman good tools.'

Some of English literature's great luminaries have agreed: ''Tis an ill workman that quarrels with his own tools' (Thomas d'Urfey, 1696); 'They say an ill workman never had good tools' (Jonathan Swift, 1738); and 'Good workmen never quarrel with their tools' (Lord Byron, 1818).

In fact, people who've screwed up have been blaming their tools (or the dog eating their homework, or their computer crashing) for so long that you may find that admitting you've made a mistake has the advantage of originality.

Beauty *is in the eye of the beholder/ There's no accounting for taste/ Love is blind*

OH, THIS IS so true – think of some of your friends' partners and some of those really unattractive politicians who have got their names into the tabloids for having extramarital affairs. Think also 'Love is blind', 'There's no accounting for taste and the rather sweet Italian version, 'A beetle is a beauty in the eyes of its mother.'

In its current wording, the saying didn't appear in written form until the nineteenth century, but the idea has been bandied about for centuries, as far back as the third century BC in Ancient Greece.

Shakespeare – a great snapper-up of popular themes (*see* 'All's well that ends well') – used the idea in *Love's Labour's Lost* ('Beauty is bought by judgement of the eye'), and 'Love is blind' was a favourite line: in *The Merchant of Venice*, to name but one, he has Jessica say, 'Love is blind and lovers cannot see.'

In *Poor Richard's Almanack* (1741), the American statesman, inventor, scientist and writer Benjamin Franklin wrote:

Beauty, like supreme dominion
Is but supported by opinion.

It seems that the theory isn't that far off the mark. Research at University College London in 2004 found that feelings of love suppressed the activity of those parts of the brain that control critical thought.

Beauty *is only skin deep*

THE EARLIEST EXAMPLE of this proverb came from the pen of Sir Thomas Overbury in 1613:

All the carnall beauty of my wife
Is but skin deep.

Hardly flattering to Lady Overbury. And remember Dorian Gray, who at the start of Oscar Wilde's novel is described as 'wonderfully handsome... there was something in his face that made one trust him at once.' This is before he turns to debauchery and crime, with the face in the portrait upstairs in the old schoolroom getting uglier and uglier as his behaviour becomes more and more heinous, although his own features remain unmarked. By the end, when the evil in his soul is finally written on his face, he is 'withered, wrinkled and loathsome of visage.' An extreme example, perhaps, but it does draw attention to the idea that while being beautiful is all very well, being nice is no bad thing either.

(*See* 'All that glitters is not gold', 'Never judge a book

by its cover' and 'The proof of the pudding is in the eating' for various other takes on the 'Don't judge by appearances' theme.)

You've made your **bed**, so you must lie in it

In Aesop's fable of the ant and the grasshopper (which dates from some time in the sixth century BC), the grasshopper sang all summer while the ants were busy collecting grain to see them through the winter. When the lean times came, the grasshopper begged the ants for some food and was told that as he had sung all summer he could dance now (and starve to death for all they cared). 'You've made your bed...' belongs to the same school of thought.

Aesop's moral praises the ants' thrift and foresight; modern parodies either show the ants feeding the grasshopper so that he can still sing and provide them (the affluent society) with entertainment; or the grasshopper getting loads of publicity as a victim of society and living comfortably on payments for selling his story for the rest of his life.

The serious version of the proverb means that you must take the consequences of your own actions; in real life we know that lots of people get away with (metaphorical) murder and that 'Life isn't fair – get used to it' may be a more practical maxim. (*See also* 'As you sow, so shall you reap'.)

Beggars *can't be choosers*

RECORDED IN JOHN Heywood's *Dialogue of Proverbs* of 1546, this phrase means that when you can't have exactly what you want, you should be satisfied with whatever you are given. Not unconnected to 'Don't look a gift horse in the mouth.'

Better *late than never*

THIS PHRASE IS sometimes used in an appreciative or congratulatory sense, but is more often a remark made to someone who has turned up late, or produced a piece of work, introduced a piece of legislation or made an apology less promptly than they might have done. Be careful to whom you say it: it dates back to classical times, but if you catch someone in the wrong mood I can't see that the fact that you are quoting Livy – *Potius sero quam numquam* – will stop them thumping you.

Better *safe than sorry*

See 'He who hesitates is lost', page 103.

Better the devil you know than the devil you don't

A COWARDLY ONE, I've always thought and Richard Taverner's 1539 translation of Erasmus's Latin phrase is sexist, too: 'An evil thing known is best. It is good keeping of a shrew that a man knoweth.' It's often the excuse people give for staying in an unsatisfactory job or relationship because they are frightened of the unknown alternative. Kylie Minogue reiterated this message in her song 'Better the Devil You Know', whose lyrics describe a woman promising to be there waiting for some dreadful man[4], ready to forgive and forget if he will only stop leaving her. Honestly, Kylie, whatever happened to Girl Power? Change those stupid locks and make him leave his key is my advice.

But one man's cowardice is another man's prudence, I guess, so although I am advocating 'Fortune favours the brave', you could equally well argue for 'Look before you leap'. As I said in the introduction to this book, you can't expect proverbs to make *all* the decisions for you.

---

4 Again!? *See* 'Alls well that ends well.'

It is **better** to travel hopefully than to arrive

THIS IS CERTAINLY true if you end up in one of those holiday resorts where the hotel hasn't been built yet; otherwise the assumption that wherever you are going is likely to be a disappointment is surely a bit gloomy. The original, penned by Robert Louis Stevenson in 1881 in *Virginibus Puerisque*, put it this way:

Little do ye know your own blessedness; for to travel hopefully is a better thing than to arrive, and the true success is to labour.

In his essay 'El Dorado' he expresses the same idea in a remarkably upbeat passage that exhorts us to take advantage of all the pleasures we may find in our journey through life:

We may study for ever, and we are never as learned as we would. We have never made a statue worthy of our dreams. And when we have discovered a continent, or crossed a chain of mountains, it is only to find another ocean or another plain upon the further side. In the infinite universe there is room for our swiftest diligence and to spare.

So keep at it.

D. H. Lawrence, you will not be surprised to hear, used the expression with reference to love, suggesting that the pleasure is in the courtship (or the chase?) rather than in attaining the desired object. But the Taoists said it most succinctly of all: 'The journey is the reward.'

A **bird** in the hand is worth two in the bush

IN THE EARLY days people sometimes said '...in the woods'; and there is a German equivalent, '"I have" is a better bird than "If I had".' In other words, it is better/safer/more sensible to be content with what you have rather than to risk it by chasing after something potentially more attractive but not guaranteed.

There are numerous variations of this proverb, going back centuries. The earliest with the current wording appears in 1781, as part of the lyrics of an English song:

Gay Strephon declares I'm the girl in his mind,
If he proves sincere, I'll be constant and kind,
He vows that tomorrow he'll make me his wife,
I'll fondly endeavour to bless him for life,
For all other swains I care not a rush,
One bird in the hand is worth two in the bush.

Nearly two hundred years earlier, the Authorized Version of the Bible (always a reliable source of pithy observations) confidently proclaimed, 'A living dog is better than a dead lion.' Earlier still, around 1530, in *The Boke of Nurture or Schoole of Good Manners*, Hugh Rhodes used different fauna for his analogy: 'A bird in hand is worth ten fly at large'; while in 1546, John Heywood, a collector of proverbs, continued the avian theme with: 'Better one bird in hand than ten in the wood.'

With more than a nod to falconry – in which a bird in the hand (the falcon) was certainly worth more than two in the bush (the prey) – many medieval public houses in England were named 'The Bird in Hand'. The idea must have crossed the Atlantic to what would later be the United States: in 1734 a small town in Pennsylvania was founded with the same name.

Birds *of a feather flock together*

WELL, YES AND no. You often see mixed flocks of gulls and if you are clever enough to be able to tell them apart you might notice rooks and jackdaws together, not to mention various types of tit interspersed with treecreepers and goldcrests. But in the metaphorical sense, what it boils down to is that most of us are happiest with our own kind.

The saying has been in use since at least the sixteenth century. In 1545, in his satire *The Rescuing of Romish Fox*, William Turner observed, 'Birds of one kind and colour flock and fly always together.'

By extension, the phrase 'of that feather' became another way of saying 'of that sort'. Here, for example, is Shakespeare in *Timon of Athens*:

I am not of that feather to shake off
My friend, when he must need me.

A noble sentiment, showing that Timon was *a friend indeed* (*see* page 90).

Once **bitten**, twice shy

THE CHINESE AND Japanese have a variant, 'One year bitten by a snake, for three years afraid of a grass rope,' while the Italians say, 'He who has scalded himself once blows the next time' or 'Even an ass will not fall twice in the same quicksand.' Another equivalent in English is 'Fool me once, shame on you; fool me twice, shame on me'; if you Google this you may find a hilarious YouTube clip of George W. Bush struggling with this sophisticated concept.

What they all mean is that we should learn by experience and not carry on doing the same stupid thing over and over again. If only life were that simple.

There is none so **blind** *as he who will not see*

RECORDED IN HEYWOOD'S *Dialogue of Proverbs* of 1546, this is less common but parallel to 'There is none so deaf as he who will not hear.' In both cases, 'will not' conveys the sense of 'is determined not to' – the other person's mind is made up and you might as well be talking to a brick wall. Which probably won't have ears (*see* page 179).

Blood *is thicker than water*

SIR WALTER SCOTT was adept at coining phrases and this could well be one of his creations. It appears in *Guy Mannering* (1815), in which he has one of the characters say (in a suitably Scots accent), 'Weel, blude's thicker than water; she's welcome to the cheeses and the hams just the same.'

In the literal sense the saying is perfectly true. But in the proverbial sense of 'family ties are stronger than any other' it's less clear cut. Some of us might wish we didn't have such ties (or any ties at all) with some members of our family. Nevertheless, it's clear that an interest in blood connections runs deep (like still waters, perhaps – *see* page 164); six million of us regularly tune in to *Who Do You Think You Are?* to watch people of varying degrees of

41

celebrity trying to trace their ancestors. Maybe our own relations are so dreadful that we cling to the hope that – like London mayor Boris Johnson – we will turn out to be descended from royalty, or at least have something interesting like a gangster, a bigamist or a grandmother who worked in a Pimm's factory lurking somewhere on the family tree.

You can't get **blood** out of a stone

THE PROVERB COLLECTOR Giovanni Torriano first recorded this in his *Second Alphabet* in 1662: 'To go about to fetch blood out of stones, viz. to attempt what is impossible.'

There's not much to say about this – it's so obviously true – and I've included it only as an excuse to mention that in America some people say you can't get blood out of a turnip. I wonder why they try – wouldn't a beetroot be more effective, if something vaguely blood-like was what you were after?

The stone or turnip in question is usually used as a metaphor for tight-fistedness, so the proverb means that you probably won't be able to borrow money from it, or even get it to pay back a loan. Which is why neither stones nor turnips score highly on those instant credit-rating tests you can do online.

Boys will be boys/
You're only young once

I PREFER THE more picturesque (and less sexist)[5] 'Wanton kittens make sober cats', but both it and 'Boys will be boys' amount to the same thing: let young people be frivolous while they are young – sow their wild oats, to use another more or less proverbial expression[6] – and they will then settle down and become sober members of society.

Maybe. But I think the 'growing old disgracefully' brigade is gathering strength. Today's wisdom is that you can stay young for as long as you like, or perhaps revert to youth (and its irresponsibilities) after your children have left home. As devotees of *The Chambers Dictionary* will know, middle age is a period 'between youth and old age, variously reckoned to suit the reckoner', which makes it official – you need never be middle-aged unless you choose to be.

'You're only young once' suggests that youth is full of opportunities that should be grasped while you have the energy and enthusiasm to grasp them, but nowadays there is a lot to be said for George Bernard Shaw's maxim: 'Youth is wasted on the young.'

5   To be fair, the Latin original uses a non-gender-specific word – it could have meant either 'boys' or 'children'. But by Victorian times, when the proverb was becoming established in English, the sexism was definitely there: little boys were allowed to run around, make a noise and get dirty and scruffy while their sisters were sitting quietly in the schoolroom sewing samplers.

6   'Proverbial expression', by the way, is something people say when they don't want to admit to using a cliché. This book, inevitably, is full of them.

Brevity *is the soul of wit*

SHAKESPEARE AGAIN: THIS is Polonius in *Hamlet*.[7] We have seen him a few scenes earlier giving endless advice to his son Laertes ('Neither a borrower nor a lender be,' and that sort of thing), starting up again and again just when we think he is finally done – a bit like Columbo coming back and saying, 'Just one more thing, ma'am.' So now, when we see him trying to explain to the king and queen that Hamlet has gone mad, we know that Shakespeare is having fun at his character's expense: Polonius wouldn't recognize brevity if you hit him over the head with it.

And this may be where the expression has its value to us today, if only those who have need of it could be made to acknowledge the fact. Sadly, I suspect it is a bit like Noël Coward's complaint after he wrote the song 'Don't Put Your Daughter on the Stage, Mrs Worthington': no mother who applied to him for help ever recognized herself as the pushy Mrs Worthington or her daughter as an under-talented ugly duckling. Similarly, if your tendency is to ramble around for a while before getting to the point, which may well not have been worth making in the first place, or to give totally uncalled-for examples that don't add anything to your argument, you're unlikely to realize how much more interesting you could be if you were only a little more succinct. I remember one fascinating occasion...

7 I told you to watch out for him, didn't I? *See* 'Actions speak louder than words'.

See what I mean?

And in case you're wondering why Polonius was advising his royal masters on the best way to tell jokes, 'wit' in the old sense referred not to wittiness but to wisdom – hence 'soul of wit' meant 'essence of wisdom'.

You can't make **bricks** without straw

ACTUALLY YOU CAN, perfectly well. The lengthy Wikipedia entry on brick doesn't even contain the word straw. It mentions clay, shale, soft slate, calcium silicate, concrete and quarried stone. Clay is normally fired at a temperature of up to 1000°C, which would surely set fire to any straw which was lying about. Calcium silicate bricks require hydrated lime; even primitive adobe bricks can be held together with dung and dried in the sun. So there are plenty of options.

The origins of the proverb lie in the Old Testament story of Moses asking Pharaoh to 'let my people go' (his people being the Children of Israel who were enslaved in Egypt, where they spent most of their waking hours making bricks... with straw). Pharaoh not only refused, but also ordered that, in punishment for their impertinent request, the Children of Israel should no longer be given straw. They would have to go out and find it for themselves but would nevertheless be expected to produce the same quota of bricks at the end of the day.[8]

Having spent a bit of time scrabbling about in the stubble, the Israelites complained to Moses, who in turn complained to God (if you are familiar with the book of Exodus you will recognize a recurring theme here). God, instead of saying, 'Oh, stop moaning, hold your bricks together with dung and leave them out in the sun for a bit,' intoned, 'I am the Lord and I will bring you out from under the burdens of the Egyptians, and I will rid you out of your bondage.' Which, in the fullness of time, he did.

The Wikipedia entry, however, doesn't mention divine intervention.

A new **broom** sweeps clean

THERE IS AN old superstition that you should sweep your house on New Year's Eve, getting rid of all the old year's dirt, then throw the old broom away and get a new one to cope with the new year's dirt. The rationale is that a new

---

8 'At the end of the day' came up in a newspaper poll recently as one of the expressions that annoyed people most. I mention it because this is a rare instance of it being used literally: the taskmasters said to the Children of Israel, 'Fulfil your works, your daily tasks, as when there was straw' and at the end of the day (i.e. in the evening) they counted the bricks. So, at the end of the day, there is a time and a place for using this turn of phrase.

broom sweeps clean, but I suspect it was a rationale dreamt up by broom manufacturers.

In its proverbial sense, the expression usually means 'We've got a new boss and a lot of us are likely to get the sack because he will want to bring in his own guys.' The Irish version of the proverb adds, '…but an old one knows the corners', suggesting that the new boss might be well advised to look before he leaps and not rush in where angels fear to tread.

Like many proverbs, this one has been around for a while. In 1546, in the *Dialogue of Proverbs*, John Heywood recorded 'Some thereto said, the green new broom sweepeth clean,' while a 1616 saying advises that one should not totally turn one's back on the past: 'New brooms sweep clean, yet old friendship still retain.' So don't place too great a value on that new green broom.

You can't have your **cake** and eat it too

OF ALL THE proverbs in this book, this is probably the one that brings the most pedants out of the woodwork. There are those who maintain that of course once you have eaten your cake you don't still have it (you've eaten it, right?); others that you can't possibly eat cake unless you have it in the first place. Then there are those who say you could start with a big cake and eat a bit of it and still have quite a lot left; or that you could eat a bit of *someone else's* cake; or that if you have cake obviously you are going to eat it – otherwise it goes stale.

So why don't we just forget about the cake analogy and settle for 'You can't have it both ways'– you can't worship God and Mammon; or court publicity and then object to the paparazzi following you about; or watch episode after episode of the same afternoon soap and complain that you're bored.

There is always **calm** after a storm

Some say there is always calm *before* a storm, but it's surely a 'glass half full, glass half empty' decision: either everything is dreadful, so it's bound to get better, or everything is fine, so it's bound to get worse.

Meteorologically, there are often a couple of days of clear, calm weather before a hurricane hits; it can also go strangely quiet as if, thanks to some unexplained sixth sense, the birds have realized a storm is coming, stopped singing and battened down their avian hatches. But this doesn't always happen: sometimes you know a storm is coming because it's dark and windy and rainy. That's weather for you.

As for calm *after* a storm, isn't that a tautology? Once the storm's over, it is by definition calm, surely? Or at least calmer than it was. But this comforting idea – that however bad it gets, it will one day be over – has endured the centuries. In the narrative poem *Piers Plowman*, written around 1377, William Langland says, 'After sharp showers … most shene [bright] is the sun.' Six hundred years later, in *Smiley's People*, John le Carré was reassuring his readers in similar vein: 'For the next two weeks nothing happened. After the storm had come the calm.' (*See also* 'The darkest hour is before the dawn.')

If the **cap** fits, wear it

THE ORIGINAL 'CAP' was a dunce's cap, so wearing it was an admission of stupidity; nowadays the proverb has the wider implication that, if you think criticism or blame that sounds general is in fact being aimed specifically at you, you're probably right. Possibly because it's all your fault.

A **cat** may look at a king

OR QUEEN, OF course. This is normally said by somebody who is determined to maintain their rights, even if they are in some way in an inferior position. Beware, though, before you assert yourself too forcefully for, as the Irish say, 'The cat has leave to look at the queen and the queen has leave to shoot it.'

In the 1650s, a man rejoicing in the name of Marchamont Nedham wrote a number of pamphlets supporting the existing republican state under Oliver Cromwell. Nedham was a notorious turncoat, switching from the Parliamentarian cause to the Royalist one and back again before going into hiding after the restoration of King Charles II. He then managed to get himself pardoned and lived another eighteen years without having his head chopped off – a remarkable achievement under the circumstances.

In case you are wondering why I mention this, it is because one of his republican pamphlets was called *A Cat May Look Upon a King*. But the proverb was at least a hundred years old by then, so it is safe to assume that Marchamont was using it in the way that a tabloid headline-writer might use it today – eye-catchingly but more or less meaninglessly.

When the **cat's** away, the mice will play

ORIGINATING IN EARLY fourteenth-century French – *ou chat na rat regne* ('where there is no cat the rat is king') – nowadays for 'cat' read 'boss' or 'random person we are scared of and who keeps us in order' and for 'mice' read 'underling' or 'any of the rest of us'. Alternatively, try 'wife' and 'potentially errant husband', because that is the sense in which the expression is most often used.

But do mice play? Whether the cat is away or not? Well, yes, according to several 'keeping mice as pets' websites. An old toilet roll tube or empty egg box can amuse them for ages. (Little things please little minds? *See* page 119.) And, like hamsters, they will run round and round in a wheel for the sheer joy of it. They love mazes and anything else of that sort that they can explore.

But if you want to ensure that they continue to frisk and frolic, keep them away from your cat.

A **change** *is as good as a rest*

THIS WAS ORIGINALLY phrased as 'a change of work is a rest'; Sir Arthur Conan Doyle used it of himself when he took a break from medicine and writing, immersed himself in chemical analysis and emerged refreshed. Well, there's no accounting for taste (*see* page 33).

Many distinguished authors have maintained that change is a good thing in itself. Voltaire wrote that 'if we do not find anything pleasant, at least we shall find something new'; the American writer Washington Irving remarked rather wryly that 'there is a certain relief in change, even though it be from bad to worse... it is often a comfort to shift one's position and be bruised in a new place'; and the philosopher Ralph Waldo Emerson took the same view, though perhaps from a loftier position: 'With consistency a great soul has simply nothing to do.'

All very well, gentlemen, but what about when you're on a horse in midstream? Not so cocky then, are you? (*See* below, and also 'Variety is the spice of life').

Don't **change** horses in midstream

... UNLESS YOU are a good rider *and* a good swimmer. This is particularly sound advice for squatters, by the way (*see* 'Possession is nine points of the law,' page 141): if you have to build up, say, ten years' adverse possession before you gain rights to the property, it's no good moving out after seven and then coming back and thinking you have only three to go. You'll have to go back to the beginning and start again, and you may well find somebody else has moved in in the meantime – and quite possibly stolen your horse.

The original comes from no less a source than Abraham Lincoln.[9] In a speech in 1864, Honest Abe advised against changing political sides and as an example recalled 'an old Dutch farmer, who remarked to a companion once that it was best not to swap horses when crossing streams...'

---

9 Someone else who, like Hamlet, will make a number of appearances in this book.

Plus ça **change**, plus c'est la même chose

THE FIRST QUESTION is, 'Why do we say it in French?' Answer: 'Because "the more it changes, the more it is the same thing" doesn't sound anything like as clever or deep.' Alternative answer: 'Because it's a quote from a Frenchman.' Put the two together and that's as close to a sensible explanation as you are going to get.

The Frenchman concerned was a nineteenth-century journalist called Alphonse Karr, founder of a paper called *Les Guêpes*, which means 'The Wasps' and which became famous for its, well, waspish humour. Karr made this, his most famous of a number of waspish remarks, in early 1849, a year after King Louis-Philippe was ousted and Louis-Napoleon established as president of the Second Republic. A descendant of the old royal family replaced by the nephew of the original Napoleon? Off with the old, on with the old, was Alphonse Karr's view.

In not seeing much difference between the old regime and the new, Alphonse Karr was more prescient than he can have realized; the Second Republic lasted just three years before Louis-Napoleon did away with it and proclaimed himself the Emperor Napoleon III.

In the contemporary political arena, the expression still has its uses and can be loosely translated into English as

53

'They're all as bad as each other' or, muttered under the breath, 'Well, I didn't bloody vote for them.'

Charity *begins at home*

IN THE EARLY days (and if you feel so inclined you can trace the origins of this proverb back to Roman times or to the New Testament), the suggestion was that you should learn charity – which could mean either good works and/or love for your fellow human beings – at home and then extend its bounty out into the world. In 1383, the theologian John Wycliffe, who first translated the Bible into English, had no doubts that 'Charity should begin at himself.'

Nowadays the saying is more commonly used as an excuse not to be generous to anyone but yourself. This cynical interpretation was obviously familiar in the seventeenth century, when the English dramatists Beaumont and Fletcher wrote, 'Charity and beating begin at home.' Similarly, in the 1770s, a character in Sheridan's *The School for Scandal* speaks of a man who believes in the sentiment of charity beginning at home and receives the reply, 'And his, I presume, is of that domestic sort which never stirs abroad at all.'

Quite.

The **child** is father of the man

WELL, CLEARLY NONSENSE on the face of it, but more sensible if you give some thought to what Wordsworth meant when he wrote it in 1807. It's from a poem called 'The Rainbow' which runs:

My heart leaps up when I behold
A rainbow in the sky:
So was it when my life began;
So is it now I am a man;
So be it when I shall grow old,
Or let me die!
The Child is father of the Man…

In other words, his heart always has leapt on these occasions and he hopes it always will. Which is fair enough – there's no reason to grow out of liking rainbows.

The Old Testament book of Proverbs phrases it thus: 'Train up a child in the way he should go: and when he is old, he will not depart from it,' but it's the same thing – once a rainbow lover, always a rainbow lover. Later on in the Bible Saint Paul says that when he became a man he put away childish things. He doesn't specifically mention rainbows, but I'm sure if he was against them he would have told us so. We should be OK.

Children *should be seen and not heard*

ACCORDING TO THIS very old saying, it used to be a 'maid' (that is, a young unmarried woman, rather than a servant) who should be careful not to put herself forward. So, unlike 'Boys will be boys', this started out as sexist and became generic, probably in Victorian times, when some upper-class parents hardly saw their children at all and, when they did, wanted them freshly scrubbed, ready for bed and firmly under the control of their nanny.

Nowadays I suppose it is a matter of taste. It's perfectly possible to adore your own children, think your friends' toddlers are hilarious, but find the noisy young strangers who run riot in your local pizza restaurant deeply annoying. Alternatively, you could just object to the whole lot of them, in which case you could fall back on the grumpy old person's cliché, 'I blame the parents' (*see* 'Spare the rod and spoil the child').

Cleanliness *is next to godliness*

IN THE EARLIEST forms of this proverb, 'next to' did not mean 'equal to' but rather 'next in line'. Francis Bacon, the seventeenth-century English statesman and philosopher, wholeheartedly agreed: 'Cleanness of body was ever esteemed to proceed from a due reverence to God.' In other words, the desire to maintain good personal hygiene was the natural outcome of being a good Christian.

If you were brought up on the cartoon strip *Peanuts,* you will probably remember the endearingly and enduringly filthy character Pig-Pen, who once remarked that for him cleanliness was next to impossible. Nowadays, when it is no great challenge to most of us to shower every day, there is probably a middle ground to be found between the holier-than-thou tone of the proverb and the clouds of dirt that followed Pig-Pen around. And we're not just talking about 'cleanliness of body': if you feel that life is too short to spend time dusting, for example, you can take comfort from the line from Christopher Fry's play *The Lady's Not for Burning,* first performed in 1948: 'What after all is a halo? It's only one more thing to keep clean.'

Every **cloud** has a silver lining

OR 'ALWAYS LOOK on the bright side of life,' as Eric Idle might have phrased it. We're back to 'glass half full, glass half empty' here, but the background to the proverb is that a dark cloud frequently reflects the light of the sun or moon behind it, giving it (the cloud) a silver edging. Leading, of course, to the metaphorical usage that says that the darkest situation has some glimmer of hope to it.

Noël Coward – that virtuoso of the world-weary approach to life – would have none of this. In his song 'There Are Bad Times Just Around the Corner', the voice of experience advises us that 'it's no good whining about a silver lining' because the dark clouds aren't going to go away.

On the other hand, a browse through the website of Gavin Pretor-Pinney's Cloud Appreciation Society might lead you to a more cheerful view.[10] The society's manifesto pledges to fight the monotony of 'blue-sky thinking' and the site contains literally hundreds of photographs of stormy cumulo-nimbus clouds, almost all of them with a silver – or gold or pink or bright, bright blue – lining. It makes you think – and that is the society's purpose – that it's worth having the clouds after all.

Cold *hands, warm heart*

Cold hands, poor blood circulation actually. You may be suffering from Raynaud's disease, which means that the small blood vessels that should let blood into your hands (and keep them warm) go into spasm and constrict. In severe cases you can have unpleasant-sounding surgery, or there is a treatment called thermal biofeedback through which you train your body to vasodilate (i.e. unconstrict the blood vessels). Or you may prefer just to keep your gloves on and put up with it.

10 www.cloudappreciationsociety.org

The expression occurs in a collection of proverbs dated 1903, and in a play by J. M. Barrie (the creator of Peter Pan) of 1927, where it is referred to as an established saying. Where it came from in the first place is anyone's guess – and there seems to be no medical evidence to support it.

Two's **company**, *three's a crowd*

ANOTHER VERSION, FOUND for example in William Hazlitt's *English Proverbs* of 1869, runs: 'Two's company, three is none.' Most courting couples would agree, though how they might feel at a later stage of their relationship is more open to debate. Oscar Wilde – or rather, his creation Algernon in *The Importance of Being Earnest* – went so far as to suggest that in married life 'three is company and two none'. But as Algy also says, 'Relations are simply a tedious pack of people, who haven't got the remotest knowledge of how to live, nor the smallest instinct about when to die' and 'The amount of women in London who flirt with their own husbands is perfectly scandalous. It looks so bad,' we may not be intended to take his views on life completely seriously.

Comparisons *are odious*

OR 'ODOROUS', AS Dogberry, one of Shakespeare's dimmer characters, says in *Much Ado About Nothing*. The saying has been around since at least the fourteenth century. All it means is that if you compare one person with another you are likely to offend at least one of them.

In Sheridan's *The Rivals*, Mrs Malaprop got it even more wrong when she rebuked her niece Lydia for maintaining that her favoured suitor is as handsome as the one her aunt prefers: 'No caparisons, Miss, if you please! Caparisons don't become a young woman.'

More seriously, Abraham Lincoln used the expression in a speech referring to those who had died at the Battle of Buena Vista during the Mexican-American War: 'In speaking of this, I mean no odious comparison between the lion-hearted whigs and democrats who fought there. I wish to do justice to all.'

A caparison, by the way, is a decorative covering for a war horse and – as so often with Mrs Malaprop – has nothing to do with the subject under discussion.

Too many **cooks** spoil the broth/ Many hands make light work

OH FOR HEAVEN'S sake, I hear you cry, who writes these things? (Actually, we're not sure in this case, but it's believed to have been coined in the late sixteenth century.) But stop and think about it for a moment, because there is a sensible demarcation here. 'Too many cooks...' is a warning against design – or in this case broth-making – by committee, whereas 'Many hands...' refers to some more menial task, such as the washing up. In which case many hands do indeed get through the job more quickly, unless the drying is being done by someone who doesn't know where anything goes.

Abraham Lincoln had a variation on this theme, though he was quoting an existing proverbial expression: 'One bad general is better than two good ones ... an army is better directed by a single mind, though inferior, than by two superior ones, at variance, and cross-purposes with each other.' Considering that he was president during the American Civil War, he was probably speaking from the heart. (*See also* 'Two heads are better than one', page 101.)

Don't **count** your chickens before they are hatched

THIS IS A quotation from Aesop's *The Milkmaid and Her Pail*, though the Lithuanians[11] have a rather picturesque variation on the theme: 'The calf isn't even born yet and there he is sharpening his carving knife.' Both versions are warnings against taking anything for granted or acting prematurely on something that may or may not happen. Because, as you know if you are reading this book alphabetically (and if you aren't, you may like to go back to page 39 at this point), a bird in the hand is worth two in the bush.

In the **country** of the blind, the one-eyed man is king

WAY BACK IN 1522, the English poet John Skelton elegantly expressed this saying thus: 'An one eyed man is Well sighted when He is among blind men.' In other words, if everyone else is really stupid or ignorant or, as P. G. Wodehouse put it, constitutionally incapable of walking through the great Gobi Desert without knocking something over, you don't have to be very bright or well informed or dextrous to come out at the top of the heap.

11 Yes, really – isn't the Internet wonderful?

The **course** of true love never did run smooth

THIS IS THAT rare creature, a quote from Shakespeare that isn't from *Hamlet*. It's Lysander talking to Hermia at the beginning of *A Midsummer Night's Dream*, bemoaning the fact that her father won't let them marry but drawing some bizarre crumb of comfort from remembering that opposition from one's nearest and dearest, disparity in age or in social class, or other such minor impediments as war, illness and death have stood in the way of lovers throughout history.[12] But, the implication is, true love will conquer all.

If you're familiar with the play, you'll know that true love did indeed conquer all, but not without the intervention of a wood full of fairies who squirted aphrodisiac juice on various people's eyelids and caused considerable confusion before they were done.

My advice is: you'll improve the odds of your love life running smooth – or smoothly, if you want to be pedantic about it – if you stay away from aphrodisiac juices. And men with asses' heads. They may both have their place on a dull Saturday night, but we're looking at long-term commitment here.

12 It's surprising, come to think of it, that Lysander doesn't mention castration in his long list of obstacles to true love: he covers just about everything else, and Shakespeare would surely have known about the grisly fate of Abelard, the lover of Eloise.

Don't **cross** your bridges before you come to them

ALTHOUGH THE FORM of words might seem similar, this is nothing to do with not counting your chickens before they're hatched. First recorded in 1850, it is more like 'Sufficient unto the day is the evil thereof' (*see* 'You can't serve God and Mammon') – in other words, don't worry about it (whatever 'it' may be) until it happens. Burning your bridges afterwards is optional.

You've got to be **cruel** to be kind

IN 1979 A singer called Nick Lowe had a minor hit with a song called *Cruel to be Kind*, a man's lament about the unkindness of his girlfriend. In response to his complaints she says, 'Cruel to be kind means that I love you', but surely this is just a pretty flagrant excuse for her messing him about? If she doesn't want him she should ditch him and have done with it – now that *would* be being cruel to be kind.

Actually Hamlet[13] said, 'I must be cruel only to be kind' a few hundred years before Nick Lowe, but Hamlet said so many things that I thought it might be interesting to talk about somebody else for a change.

13 Remember him?

Parents wanting to justify being cruel to be kind should look up 'Spare the rod and spoil the child.'

It's no use **crying** over spilt milk

BECAUSE CRYING WON'T put it back in the bottle, nor make the floor any less sticky if you don't wipe it up properly. Confucius phrases it, 'Things that are done, it is needless to speak about ... things that are past, it is needless to blame' and, as so often, he is quite right. If you aren't as nice a person as Confucius, however, check out 'Revenge is a dish best served cold.'

Curiosity killed the cat

NONSENSE, OF COURSE: there are no recorded incidences of curiosity being fatal, to cats or anyone else, unless it caused them to cross the road without looking both ways. It's another of those 'nannyisms' such as 'Children should be seen and not heard' or 'Ask no questions and you'll be told no lies' – in this case intended to chastise inquisitive youngsters.

In the original version, however, 'care' (in the sense of 'worry'), not curiosity, was what dealt the fatal blow. In his play of 1598, *Every Man in his Humour*, Ben Jonson recorded the expression for the first time when he had a character say: 'Helter skelter, hang sorrow, care'll kill a Cat, up-tails all, and a Louse for the Hangman.' Among the actors who performed the play was one William Shakespeare. He must have liked the saying, because it pops up the following year in *Much Ado About Nothing*: 'What, courage man! what though care killed a cat, thou hast mettle enough in thee to kill care.' And care – not curiosity – was still killing cats as late as the latter half of the nineteenth century.

It was probably cats' notorious inquisitiveness that led to the change from 'care' to 'curiosity', and the current wording of the rather preachy proverb that we know now.

The **darkest** hour is before the dawn

THE INTERNET IS full of weird and wonderful information about how science works, but with this one it surpassed itself, guiding me to an issue of the *Monthly Weather Review* dated August 1914. This quotes a Mr Denning of Liverpool, 'a well-known observer of meteors', who had written in with his thoughts on the subject:

Before dawn a greater darkness seems to drop down like a mantle upon the immediate surroundings. Objects which were plainly observable during the previous hours of the night are blotted out, and a nervous feeling is sometimes induced by the dense opacity of the air. I think the unusual darkness only lasts a short time, and that a quick brightening succeeds, but its occurrence is most marked and by no means a rare experience...

I regret that I have recorded no observations in detail, and so can not say the exact interval before sunrise when the remarkable darkness came on, and whether it is common to every night and season and condition of sky. But of its frequent manifestation I can speak with confidence.

Sweet, but not very scientific: all the experts will tell you that the darkest hour is halfway between sunset and sunrise. Nevertheless, the proverb has been around since the seventeenth century and has been the inspiration for lots of songs, from country and western to indie rock, all of them saying that things will get better if you hang in there.

Desperate *situations call for desperate measures*

THIS ORIGINALLY HAD a medical connection (you still sometimes hear the variant 'desperate remedies') and – guess what? – in that guise it crops up in *Hamlet*.[14] Claudius, the usurping king, is justifying (to himself – nobody else would be fooled for a minute) his plan to exile Hamlet:

14 Are you keeping count?

Diseases desperate grown
By desperate appliance are relieved
Or not at all.

In other words, Hamlet is becoming a problem so let's send him away, maybe have him murdered, what do you reckon, a man's gotta do what a man's gotta do, etc. (*See* 'Needs must when the devil drives' for another way of expressing the same sentiments.)

The **devil** finds work for idle hands

THE WELSH SAY, 'The seed of all evil is laziness', the Italians, 'An idle man is the devil's bolster' and the Germans, 'The devil dances in an empty pocket', but they all mean the same thing: keep yourself busy or you'll get into mischief. No less a person than Saint Jerome warned of this pitfall in his *Letters: Fac et aliquid operis, ut semper te diabolus inveniat occupatum*. For those of us who can't read Latin, Chaucer helpfully paraphrased the holy man in 1386, in *The Tale of Melibee* from his *Canterbury Tales*: 'Dooth somme goode dedes that the devel, which is oure enemy, ne fynde yow nat unoccupied.' That's perfectly clear then.

The devil features in a lot of proverbs: in addition to the ones listed in this book (*see* 'Better the devil you know than the devil you don't', 'Talk/speak of the devil and he will appear' and 'Needs must when the devil drives') there are:

- 'The devil can quote scripture for his own ends' – said of someone who is clever at twisting words.

- 'The devil is not as black as he is painted' – nonsense, surely, because if you allow that 'black' in this context means 'evil', what is the point of a devil who is not as evil as he is made out to be?

- 'The devil looks after his own' and 'The devil's children have the devil's own luck' – people who do well in this world have sold their soul to the devil.

- 'The devil sick would be a monk' – said of someone who makes fervent promises of the 'Get me out of this and I'll be good' kind, then forgets them as soon as the difficulty is past.

- 'The devil gets into the belfry in the priest's cassock' – a Spanish proverb presumably casting aspersions on the morality of the clergy.

- 'The devil catches most souls in a golden net' – meaning something along the lines of Christ's warning that it is easier for a camel to pass through the eye of a needle than for a rich man to enter the kingdom of God.

- 'The devil's boots don't creak' – a Scottish saying suggesting that temptation can creep up on you without your realizing it.

- 'The devil makes his Christmas pies of lawyers' tongues and clerks' fingers' – a wonderful piece of imagery popular in the sixteenth century when it was sometimes said that the devil also used a third ingredient in his cooking: women.

- 'Why should the devil have all the best tunes?' An excellent question initially posed by either the early Methodist hymn writer Charles Wesley or the evangelist Rowland Hill, both of whom maintained that it wasn't absolutely essential for hymns to be dreary. And it raises the further question, 'Why should the devil have all the best proverbs?'

Discretion *is the better part of valour*

THIS IS A very Aristotelian concept – Aristotle reckoned that happiness was to be found at the midpoint between two extremes. Cowardice is undeniably bad, but courage (valour), taken to extremes, is foolhardy. Funny, then, that these words should have been popularized by one of the great cowards in literature – Falstaff, who speaks them (in Shakespeare's *Henry IV, Part I*) when he has just saved

his own life in a fight by falling down and pretending to

be dead.[15]

Not many people would take Falstaff as a role model, unless they wanted to get into the *Guinness Book of Records* for sack drinking, but Aristotle was no fool and it's always worth giving a bit of respect to his ideas.

Distance *lends enchantment*

OR, THINGS LOOK better from far away, as the Scottish poet Thomas Campbell said in his best-selling *The Pleasures of Hope* in 1799:

Why do those cliffs of shadowy tint appear
More sweet than all the landscape smiling near? —
'Tis distance lends enchantment to the view,
And robes the mountain in its azure hue.

The proverb is a variation on 'Absence makes the heart grow fonder' and from the same school of thought as 'Familiarity breeds contempt': when your loved one is at a distance, it's easy to overlook the mundane details of their snoring, and to focus on the magical qualities that made you fall in love with them in the first place. That's assuming you can remember what they were.

---

15 He phrases it 'The better part of valour is discretion,' but let's not quibble.

Do unto others as you would have them do unto you

Here's a great quote from Abraham Lincoln:

When, a year or two ago, those professedly holy men of the South, met in the semblance of prayer and devotion, and, in the name of Him who said 'As ye would all men should do unto you, do ye even so unto them' appealed to the Christian world to aid them in doing to a whole race of men, as they would have no man do unto themselves, to my thinking, they contemned and insulted God and His church, far more than did Satan when he tempted the Saviour with the Kingdoms of the earth. The devil's attempt was no more false, and far less hypocritical.

This is a rant against the concept of slavery, but the principle of 'do as you would be done by' is much older than that: you can find it in Confucius and in Hindu, Jewish and Christian teaching. Charles Kingsley's novel *The Water-Babies* — an archetypally Victorian moral tale — features a pair of sisters called Mrs Doasyouwouldbedoneby, who is sweet and kind and loving, and Mrs Bedonebyasyoudid, who brings retribution to those who deserve it.

In this day and age, Victorian moral tales are rather out of fashion and 'Do unto others before they do you'[16] may seem a more streetwise attitude.

16 Even that isn't new. Dickens used it in *Martin Chuzzlewit*, but not as a piece of advice from author to reader — the speaker is Jonas Chuzzlewit, who is up there with Bill Sikes as one of Dickens's out-and-out bad guys.

Give a **dog** a bad name and hang him

RECORDED IN 1706 as 'Give a dog an ill name and his work is done,' this is one of those proverbs where the terseness of the wording makes it less easy to understand: 'If you give a dog a bad name, you might as well hang him while you're at it' would be clearer, but proverbs are always inclined to favour pithiness over clarity.

Anyway, mud sticks is what it means (*see* 'Fling enough dirt and some will stick'). If a dog – or anyone else – gets a bad reputation, they're likely to be assumed guilty when the next piece of gossip comes along.

There are lots of good quotes about gossip and scandal, of which my all-time favourite is said to have been embroidered on a cushion belonging to the American society hostess Alice Roosevelt Longworth, daughter of President Theodore Roosevelt: 'If you haven't got anything good to say about anyone, come and sit by me.' Napoleon was more selective about his gossip: 'It is a matter of great interest what sovereigns are doing; but as to what Grand Duchesses are doing – who cares?' You can tell he lived in the days before tabloid newspapers and reality TV. Hamlet,[17] as you might expect, is more morose: 'Be thou as chaste as ice, as pure as snow, thou shalt not escape calumny.'

17 Sorry, I did warn you.

Now that's a depressing thought: the mud is going to stick whether you do anything improper or not. It's enough to make you think, 'Well, might as well be hanged for a sheep as for a lamb.' (*See* page 100)

A **drowning** man will clutch at a straw

In other words, you have to do whatever is necessary to get yourself out of a desperate situation (but you're still likely to fail). The Italians are even more drastic – they say he'll clutch at a razor. In the English version, the clutching won't achieve anything, in the Italian it'll hurt like hell; either way it suggests you are running out of options. And 'clutch' is certainly more suggestive of desperation than the earlier 'catch'.

Sir Thomas More, English scholar and Catholic martyr who fell foul of Henry VIII and paid with his life, must have known a thing or two about grabbing for the nearest bit of flotsam. In 1534, while in prison, he wrote *A Dialogue of Comfort Against Tribulation*, in which he mused: 'Like a man that in peril of drowning catcheth whatsoever cometh next to hand ... be it never so simple a stick.'

The **early** bird catches the worm

EARTHWORMS ARE NOCTURNAL, or at least they are light-sensitive, so they prefer to be out and about at night and on cloudy days. If you are a diurnal bird, therefore, you probably do have to get up early to catch them before them disappear for the day. In the proverbial sense, this means 'Don't delay in going for your goals; get there before someone else beats you to it.'

On a slightly higher plain, there is a Latin proverb, 'Dawn is the friend of Muses', suggesting that poets and the like should get up early in order to seek inspiration. If you are a poet who happens not to be an early riser, take comfort in Gray's 'Elegy Written in a Country Churchyard', Keats's 'Ode to a Nightingale' and Walter de la Mare's 'The Listeners',[18] all of which find something to rhapsodize about later in the day. Maybe they were right – the *Washington Post* of 4 September 2001 quoted US comedian Steven Wright, who counselled caution against too much haste in the pursuit of success: 'The early bird may get the worm, but it's the second mouse that gets the cheese.'

---

18 That's the one that begins ' "Is there anybody there?" said the Traveller,/ Knocking on the moonlit door.'

Early to bed, early to rise, makes a man healthy, wealthy and wise

THIS SAYING DATES back to the days when working hours were dictated by the amount of daylight available. One of the earliest versions, dating from 1496 and in almost impenetrable early English, reads: 'Who soo woll ryse erly shall be holy helthy and zely [lucky].' In the old days, this made perfect sense. Lying in bed after daybreak cost you valuable work time; staying up late meant spending hard-earned cash on candles or gas lamps; and for these reasons following the sun was a wise thing to do.

Although the advent of electric light has reduced the potency of the 'wealthy' and 'wise' arguments, the 'healthy' one remains valid, for genuine physiological reasons. When it gets dark, our levels of the sleep hormone melatonin rise and those of the stress-related hormone cortisol lower, making it easier for us to unwind and go to sleep. Artificial light disrupts this natural pattern, which means that if we feel like it we can work until midnight or party till two in the morning, but in so doing we lessen the body's ability to cope with stress and with general wear and tear, both physical and psychological. So it really *is* healthier to sleep between 10.30 p.m. and 5.30 a.m., just the way all those annoying people who find it easy to get up in the morning have always said it is.

Easier *said than done*

YOU COULD ARGUE that 'Easier said than done' doesn't deserve to be counted as a proverb at all: if you are, for example, being advised by your doctor to lose weight or to give up smoking, it is, sadly, a statement of fact. The expression has, however, been around for over 2,000 years.

The Latin dramatist Terence, writing in the second century BC, produced what might now be called a commonplace book – a collection of thoughts and jottings; in Latin books of this kind rejoiced in the name of *Vulgaria*. In 1483, some kind soul translated it and included the expression 'It is easyer to saye than to do', the proverb's first recorded appearance in English. Back in Ancient Rome, a century after Terence, Cicero wrote 'Deeds are harder than words' in a letter to his brother. He makes this sound like a set phrase, so it seems safe to assume that the concept was nearing cliché status even then.

Easy *come, easy go*

USUALLY SAID ABOUT money and accompanied by a shrug of the shoulders – no doubt a Gallic shrug in the case of an early fifteenth-century version of the saying, which translates as, 'Soon acquired, soon spent'. Whether you're talking about money or some other substance or indeed person, the message here is: whatever arrives in your life easily and without much effort is unlikely to have staying power and will disappear as easily as it came. Elvis Presley made a film called *Easy Come, Easy Go*, about a frogman salvaging a treasure from a wreck off the California coast. *Halliwell's Film Guide* dismisses it as 'an empty-headed star vehicle' – a review that I dare say Elvis greeted with his own hip-swivelling take on the Gallic shrug.

You've got to **eat** a peck of dirt before you die

A PECK IS a more or less forgotten measure of dry goods, the equivalent of a quarter of a bushel. That's not very helpful, is it, because if you don't know what a peck is, chances are you don't know what a bushel is either. A peck is about 16 pints or just over 9 litres. That's a lot of dirt.

Taken literally, the proverb is intended to console you on, perhaps, finding a speck of dust in your tea or a smidgen of soil on your salad: never mind, it says, it won't kill you; in fact it'll probably do wonders for your immune system. Of course you might feel differently if you found a whole peck of dirt on a single plate.

The proverb has been around in this literal sense for hundreds of years; John Keats also used it figuratively, in a letter of 1819, meaning that you can't get through life without some hardship, or make an omelette without breaking eggs (*see* page 135): 'This is the second black eye I have had since leaving school … we must eat a peck before we die.'

Don't put all your **eggs** in one basket

AN EARLY EXAMPLE of this phrase can be found in Torriano's *Italian Proverbial Phrases* as 'To put all ones Eggs in a Paniard, *viz.* to hazard all in one bottom'. In other words, don't put all your hopes and effort into a single venture; spread your risk. When, in the 1980s, the pharmaceutical company Glaxo launched the antacid drug Zantac, observers worried that it was not following this maxim and was definitely putting all its eggs in one basket: what, they asked, would happen when the patent ran out and Glaxo's competitors could start producing a similar and possibly cheaper product? Answer: by the time that happened, Glaxo had merged with a couple of rivals, more than doubled its contingent of research scientists working on new products and kept motoring along very successfully, thank you.

It also marketed Zantac so vigorously that it went on to become possibly the best-selling licensed pharmaceutical of all time and, by the time its patent expired, was a very powerful brand. The company also produced a milder, over-the-counter version that kept the name in the public eye.

So, as someone at Glaxo apparently said at the time of the launch, if you do have to put all your eggs in one basket, make sure you take very good care of the basket. Towards the end of the nineteenth century Mark Twain had taken the same view: 'Behold, the fool saith, "Put not all thine eggs in the one basket" – which is but a manner of saying, "Scatter your money and your attention"; but the wise man saith, "Put all your eggs in the one basket and – watch that basket."'

An **elephant** never forgets

SCIENTIFIC OBSERVATION OF elephants has shown that they do indeed have phenomenal memories. In the Amboseli area of Kenya, inhabited by the most studied elephant population in the world, their migration patterns are reckoned to be as old as Masai oral history (that translates as 'pretty darned old', in case you aren't an aficionado of television wildlife programmes). In Botswana, elephants will travel literally hundreds of kilometres to feast on the fruit of the mokolwane palm, so I think we can assume that they remember the way. Then there are the 'elephant graveyards' we hear so much about – the legend that generation after generation of elephants returns to the same place to die. If you've seen *The Lion King* you'll know all about this. And finally, elephants are very long-lived and their social structure means that much wisdom is passed down from generation to generation, so the collective memory of a herd is considerable.

All of which is all very well, but is it any use as a proverb? Arguably not, because there is a risk that being impressed by elephants' memories we end up missing the point. The Ancient Greeks had a saying that might have been the precursor of this one: 'The camel never forgets an injury,' and in 1910 the short-story writer Saki (in *Reginald on Besetting Sins*) offered his own (somewhat sexist) take on the same idea: 'Women and elephants never forget an injury.' Both these versions suggest that the original proverb was a warning against those whose powers of recall are focused on past slights and wrongs.

An **Englishman's** home is his castle

NOW THIS IS interesting: a proverb that is just plain wrong. Back in the seventeenth century, Sir Edward Coke insisted: 'The house of everyone is to him as his castle and fortress, as well as for his defence against injury and violence as for his repose.' And he would know, because he became Lord Chief Justice of England. But nowadays, the idea that 'an Englishman's home is inviolable, no one has the right to intrude into it', simply isn't true. All sorts of people from the fire brigade to the VAT inspector have the right to stroll into your gaff, whether it be castle, bedsit or anything in-between. Often they will need a warrant, but even so...

Enough *is as good as a feast*

THIS IS A counsel against greed in favour of being content with what you have. But when they invented this proverb in the Middle Ages, they probably didn't know that it took fifteen minutes for the brain to process the information that the stomach was full, so they just kept eating until they were stuffed. The way most of us do to this day. If you are self-disciplined you stop eating *before* you feel full, but what I want to know is: how do you know *when* to stop? If you stop before you're full, how do you know how you are going to feel in fifteen minutes' time? You might not be full at all, and then what do you do? It turns every meal into a Chinese takeaway – twenty minutes later you want another one – and that can't be good for you.

To **err** *is human, to forgive divine*

THIS IS A quote from Alexander Pope's *Essay on Criticism*, published in 1711, when the poet was twenty-three. It is what's called a didactic poem and it's written with all the confidence (some would say arrogance) of youth, laying down the law about how poetry should be written, read and understood. This line comes at the end of a stanza about the evils of seeking what Pope calls 'the Sacred Lust of praise': authors who long for praise and non-authors who turn into harsh critics all run the risk of forgetting to be good people. So the point of the quotation is not that forgiving is God's prerogative and we shouldn't encroach on his territory; it is that the *ability* to forgive is a divine attribute to which we mere mortals should aspire.

By the way, Pope had a good ear for a soundbite: *The Essay on Criticism* is full of quotable remarks like this. *See* 'Fools rush in where angels fear to tread' and 'A little learning is a dangerous thing' for two others.

Every *little helps*

THIS HAS A similar meaning to 'Take care of the pennies and the pounds will take care of themselves' (*see* page 139) – in other words, small bits of thrift and saving will mount up.

The proverb becomes more fun if you go back to the longer, sixteenth-century version: 'Every little helps, said the ant, pissing into the sea at midday.' Later versions mention a wren rather than an ant, but either way the point is that the liquid contribution is minimal.

Everything *comes to those who wait*

WITH ITS ORIGINS in the sixteenth century, this is another nonsensical one, because some things will never come however long you wait. A big lottery win, for instance, or a

French lieutenant – remember Meryl Streep waiting vainly on the quayside for her lover to return? What the proverb means, of course, is 'Patience is a virtue' (*see* page 135 for a longer discussion on whether or not that is true).

The **exception** proves the rule

'PROVES' IN THIS contest means 'tests, checks to see if it works' and *Brewer's Dictionary of Phrase and Fable* explains it by saying that the very fact that an exception exists tests the validity of the rule. This doesn't make sense to me. Doesn't the existence of an exception simply invalidate the rule?

Sherlock Holmes, never one to toe the party line, would agree. In *The Sign of Four* he rebukes Watson for remarking that a client is a very attractive woman, saying that he (Holmes) never allows such personal considerations to interfere with his judgement.

'In this case, however…' says Watson.
'I never make exceptions,' insists Holmes. 'An exception disproves the rule.'

Watson marries the woman anyway, so the course of true love overcame the objections of his bossy friend.

Never mind. 'The exception proves the rule' is now hardly

ever used in the correct sense (perhaps other people didn't understand it either) and is merely said when something out of the ordinary happens. And if you do happen to believe that there are no absolute rules, 'There is no rule without an exception' – which also has a long pedigree – expresses it better, I think.

What the **eye** doesn't see, the heart doesn't grieve over

RECORDED AS HAVING been quoted by Saint Bernard in the early fourteenth century, this is cynical but true. If you don't know about it, you can't be upset about it. (*See also* 'Where ignorance is bliss, 'tis folly to be wise.')

Faint heart never won fair lady

See 'Nothing ventured, nothing gained', page 134.

Familiarity breeds contempt

ANOTHER ONE OF Aesop's (*see* 'You've made your bed, so you must lie in it', 'Look before you leap', 'Slow but steady wins the race' and 'United we stand, divided we fall'), this time the moral of an odd little story about a fox who was initially very scared of a lion but gradually got used to having him around and 'passed the time of day with him, asking him how his family were, and when he should have the pleasure of seeing him again; then turning his tail, he parted from the Lion without much ceremony.' Not really contemptuous, I wouldn't have thought – and I'd also have found it more interesting if the lion had eaten the fox at the end of it all.

Fine *words butter no parsnips*

See 'Actions speak louder than words', page 24.

Fling *enough dirt and some will stick*

THIS IS A variation on the theme of 'Give a dog a bad name and hang him' or 'There's no smoke without fire': if you abuse someone thoroughly enough, their reputation will be sullied. I have seen this attributed to the Italian statesman Machiavelli and, although I can't find the original, the satirical writer Edward Ward picked up on the Machiavellian slant in his *Hudibras Redivivus*, a 'burlesque poem on the times' (1705):

Scurrility's a useful Trick
Approv'd by the most Politic;
Fling Dirt enough,
And some will stick.

If Machiavelli didn't say something like that, he certainly ought to have done.

A **fool** and his money are soon parted

IT WAS EVER thus. Writing in his *Five Hundred Points of Good Husbandry* back in 1573, Thomas Tusser gave us this warning in rhyme: 'A fool and his money be soon at debate: which after with sorrow repents him too late.'

Nothing much has changed since then and it's a fate that isn't restricted to fools: the most prudent and provident among us have been being parted from their money on a regular basis ever since Robert Maxwell went over the side of his yacht in 1991.

Only **fools** and horses work

IF YOU'RE SMART, this rather world-weary proverb says, you'll find ways of bringing in the money without resorting to hard graft. Nigel Rees's collection of homely sayings *All Gong and No Dinner* gives an even more sardonic alternative: 'Only fools and horses work, and horses turn their back on it'; Rees also suggests that the saying makes more sense if it is expanded to 'Only fools and horses work for nothing.' Nowadays some might maintain that, with our pensions and savings vanishing into thin air, we've been doing that anyway…

Fools *rush in where angels fear to tread*

ALEXANDER POPE AGAIN, in his *Essay on Criticism* (*see* 'To err is human, to forgive divine' and 'A little learning is a dangerous thing'). This line comes at the end of a verse that refers to:

The Bookful Blockhead, ignorantly read,
With Loads of Learned Lumber in his Head.

Such a person, Pope says, is only too ready to criticize everything he has read, while wiser critics will express themselves with 'modest Caution'. When I was a student I had a poster on my wall that said, 'Oh Lord, help me to keep my big mouth shut until I know what I am talking about.' It's the same idea and I'm still working on it.

Forewarned *is forearmed*

MEANING THAT IF you know something is coming you can prepare for it, this saying has been around since at least the sixteenth century. Even earlier, the Romans, always a rich source of wise saws, provided their own take on the idea: *Praemonitus, praemunitus.*

This is the reason they tell you at the beginning of the year that you have exams at the end of it, just in case you feel like doing any work for them.

Fortune *favours the brave*

See 'Nothing ventured, nothing gained', page 134.

A **friend** *in need is a friend indeed*

THOSE WHO PREFER 'A friend in need is a pest' or any of the many other misanthropic variations are – probably wilfully – missing the point. The proverb means 'A friend who is a friend to you when you are in need is truly a friend', which I admit doesn't exactly trip off the tongue. Nevertheless it has an ancient pedigree and has earned widespread recognition: Publilius Syrus, a Roman writer of the first century BC, said, 'Prosperity makes friends, adversity tries [i.e. tests] them', and both French and Bulgarian have equivalent sayings.

Various maxims also remind us that friendship is a two-way street, including the Turkish 'A wise man remembers his friends at all times; a fool, only when he has need of them' and the Scandinavian 'Go often to the house of a friend; for weeds soon choke up the unused path.'

It's easy to poke fun at friendship; it's also easy to be schmaltzy and the dictionaries of quotations are full of examples of both. But here's one that gives pause for thought, courtesy of the late, great Spike Milligan: 'Money couldn't buy friends, but you got a better class of enemy.'

Give *a man enough rope and he'll hang himself*

MANY COUNTRY AND western songs have absurdly long, often punning titles, such as 'I Gave Her My Heart and a Diamond and She Clubbed Me with A Spade' and 'Get Off the Table, Mabel (the $2 is for the Beer)', but perhaps the all-time best is 'She Gave Him Enough Rope to Hang Himself and He's Still Out There Swinging' (*see* 'When the cat's away the mice will play' and 'What's sauce for the goose is sauce for the gander' for other examples of what the proverb-writers believe happens when men aren't kept under strict control).

Away from the twanging guitars and lovelorn drawl, this proverb is quoted in T. Fuller's *Holy War* (1647): 'They were suffered to have rope enough, till they had haltered themselves.' It is a warning against giving someone too much freedom (they're bound to get themselves into trouble) or an incentive to delegate to an inefficient colleague (they're bound to make a mess of things and make you look good).

You can't serve **God** and Mammon

THIS IS A Christian maxim, taken from the Sermon on the Mount – that's the one where Christ said, 'Blessed are the meek, for they shall inherit the Earth ... as long as no one else minds.'[19]

Mammon, according to *Collins English Dictionary*, is 'the personification of riches and greed in the form of a false god' and the proverb means that you should concentrate on God and righteousness, and let worldly matters take care of themselves. Indeed, worrying about worldly matters is futile, Jesus says ('Which of you by taking thought can add one cubit unto his stature?'), because God will look after you ('Consider the lilies of the field, how they grow; they toil not, neither do they spin') and tomorrow will take care of itself ('Sufficient unto the day is the evil thereof'). That's four really good quotes within eleven verses: not

19 Yes, I know, but he did say some of it.

bad for someone who didn't, so far as we know, employ a speech-writer.

Actually, there's a fifth, because before any of the rest he says, 'No man can serve two masters' and anyone who has tried it even in a secular sense is likely to agree that having more than one boss is – perhaps appropriately – hell on earth.

God *helps those who help themselves*

THIS IS A proverb that gives plenty of scope for irreverent variations – '...but we prosecute' is sometimes seen in shops to discourage shoplifters. 'God help those caught helping themselves' may have the same meaning, or may simply be designed to deter children from raiding the biscuit tin.

What it means, though – in secular terms – is not much more than 'You make your own luck', or 'If you want results, you've got to take action'. Aeschylus, the Ancient Greek playwright, maintained, 'God likes to assist the man who toils,' while in early fifteenth-century French the saying went *Aidez vous, Dieu vos aidera* or 'Help yourself, God will help you'. The National Lottery picks up the theme, enticing hopefuls with the slogan, 'You've got to be in it to win it.' There's an old joke that puts it in the proverbial nutshell: a man prayed week after week that he would win the lottery and in the end God said to him, 'For heaven's sake, give me some help – buy a ticket.'

Whom the **gods** love dies young

THIS IS A quote from an Ancient Greek playwright called Menander and refers to the story of a mother who prayed to the goddess Hera to heap the greatest possible blessings on the head of her two sons. Hera had them die in their sleep and presumably wafted them off to Heaven (or laughed up her sleeve at how stupid mortals can be).

Ever since then the expression has been trotted out by way of consolation on the occasion of a premature death. But when you consider that Bonnie and Clyde, who were really quite bad people, were both dead by the time they were twenty-five, while James Stewart lived to be eighty-nine (and the gods loved him, surely? Everyone else did), you might conclude that over the centuries we have accorded proverbial status to a pretty meaningless generalization.

What **goes** around comes around

WELL, IT'S THE title of a song by Justin Timberlake,[20] and I *think* his lyrics mean that his girlfriend has been nasty to him but she'd better watch out because one day someone will be nasty to her. Which is one take on the proverb.

In a bloodier vein, but with the same emphasis on retribution, the *Oxford Dictionary of Proverbs* quotes a 1989 *Washington Times* report on the French Revolution: 'No sooner had the royal accusers sent Louis XVI and his queen to the guillotine, than they themselves were being hoist onto the tumbrels by men whose own heads would later drop into the basket. What goes around comes around.'[21]

Another interpretation is the more relaxed 'Easy come, easy go' (*see* page 78) or, if you're more Doris Day than Justin Timberlake, 'Que será será'.

One **good** turn deserves another

DATING BACK TO the early fourteenth century, this is another proverb that can be taken either way. It could

---

20 Impressed? Not only have I heard of Justin Timberlake, I listened to the song on YouTube. Twenty-first century, here I come.

21 It was the two-hundredth anniversary. There is no suggestion that this distinguished publication was reporting Marie Antoinette's execution as if it were news.

simply be expressing a desire to return a favour done with no expectation of reward – one generous, unselfish act inviting another in return; or it could have undertones of a *quid pro quo* along the lines of 'You owe me' or 'You scratch my back and I'll scratch yours', which makes it clear that something underhand is going on.

Good *wine needs no bush*

THIS MIGHT HAVE been the motto of Spiderman or Superman (*see* 'Noblesse oblige') if they'd thought of it: it means that if you have a good product, you don't need to shout about it. (The bush in question, by the way, was an arrangement of vine leaves and ivy that served as an inn sign in Roman times.) Shakespeare picked up the idea and ran with it in *As You Like It*: 'If it be true that good wine needs no bush, 'tis true that a good play needs no epilogue.'

However, I doubt if this proverb would cut much ice in today's marketing-mad world, particularly now that wine has become so complicated (and there is far more to choose from in the supermarket than Blue Nun). So this is one of the few sayings that is genuinely obsolete – it has been replaced by 'It pays to advertise.'

The **grass** is always greener on the other side of the fence

PETULA CLARK HAD a hit with a song called 'The Other Man's Grass Is Always Greener', in which she warned people who were always longing to change their lives that they'd be better off being contented with their lot.[22] In fact Pet Clark sang a lot of cheerful, bouncy songs that were full of good advice – don't sleep in the subway, go downtown and forget all your troubles, you can colour my world with sunshine – all very sensible and this is no exception. You can waste a lot of time coveting your neighbour's house, ox, manservant, wife or, in this case, lawn.

Speaking of coveting your neighbour's wife, though, there is a classical precedent to this proverb: the Roman poet Ovid said, 'The crop is always better in another man's field; his cows are richer in milk.' This was in his poem *Ars Amatoria* – 'The Art of Love' – which is about what one might euphemistically describe as dalliance, so he wasn't really talking about crops and cows. But a word of warning here: *Ars Amatoria* got Ovid exiled to a gloomy place by the Black Sea for the rest of his life, so this is probably not an example to be followed.

---

22 It got to Number Twenty in 1967, so there's no need to feel bad if you missed it.

Half *a loaf is better than no bread*

APHRA BEN, AN unusual person in that she was not only a spy for King Charles II but also a playwright – and, heaven forbid, a woman too – wrote a comedy entitled *The Rover*. In this, one character offers another the following take on this proverb: 'You know the Proverb of the half Loaf, Ariadne, a Husband that will deal thee some Love is better than one who can give thee none.' In other words, girl, settle for what you can get …

The **hand** *that rocks the cradle rules the world*

THIS COMES FROM a poem by the nineteenth-century American poet William Ross Wallace:

They say that man is mighty,
He governs land and sea,
He wields a mighty sceptre
O'er lesser powers that be;
But a mightier power and stronger
Man from his throne has hurled,
And the hand that rocks the cradle
Is the hand that rules the world.

The hand that does the rocking is most likely that of

your mother, but the quotation means more than 'You should listen to what she says'; it suggests that the maternal influence runs so deep that it continues to affect people throughout life, and thus shapes society.

In the 1992 film of this name, the hand that rocked the cradle was a crazed nanny who may not have ruled the world but certainly gave the local Neighbourhood Watch something to think about.

Many **hands** make light work

See 'Too many cooks spoil the broth', page 62.

Handsome is as handsome does

First recorded in A. Munday's *View of Sundry Examples* in 1580, this is another variation on the theme of beauty being only skin deep – however fabulous you may look on the outside, the way you behave towards others is more important.

Flicking through reference books looking for something to give another slant on this proverb, I came across, 'Fame vaporizes, money goes with the wind, and all that's left is character.' A noble sentiment, neatly phrased – what more could you want from a quotation? Answer: the fact that this appears to have been said by, of all people, O. J. Simpson. My cup runneth over.

You might as well be **hanged** for a sheep as for a lamb

PUT IN THE word 'stealing' after the first 'for' and this makes more sense. It dates, obviously, from the days when capital punishment was meted out for all sorts of trivial offences and the implication is that if you are going to be hanged anyway you might as well do something *really* bad. Nowadays, when you are unlikely to be hanged for stealing anything, the expression has more of a shoulder-shrugging, 'what the hell?' feel to it, along the lines of 'In for a penny, in for a pound' (*see* page 139).

More **haste**, less speed

THE LATIN EQUIVALENT is *Festina lente* or 'Hasten slowly' – a variation on 'If a job's worth doing, it's worth doing well' and 'Rome wasn't built in a day.' Fittingly, therefore, it is said to have been a favourite saying of the Emperor Augustus, who also favoured 'Better a safe commander than a bold' and 'That is done quickly enough which is done well enough.' A prudent man, Augustus: he compared going into battle without being confident of victory to fishing with a golden hook, 'the loss of which, if it were carried off, could not be made good by any catch.'

Most of us aren't going into battle as part of our daily routine, but we are still familiar with the irritating way the duvet fights back when we are trying to change the bedlinen in a hurry. As so often with proverbs, the principle is the same whether we are talking large scale or small.

Two **heads** are better than one

WELL, PRESUMABLY ZAPHOD Beeblebrox thought so, and according to the BBC's *Hitchhiker's Guide to the Galaxy* website he is 'so cool you could keep a side of meat in him for a month'. On the other hand, he is consistently voted the Worst Dressed Sentient Being in the Known Universe, so you may or may not choose to make him your role model.

In the less literal sense, and like the less well-known 'Four eyes see better than two', this proverb extols the benefits of having someone else help you make up your mind – and it's a view that goes back to at least the fourteenth century. But while it is always useful to have a second opinion (a sounding board? someone else to blame?) it might also be worth bearing in mind the disadvantages of design or decision-making by committee: something that pleases everyone really pleases no one. So whereas two heads may well be better than one, three could be a crowd.

Hell *hath no fury like a woman scorned*

NOT A BIBLICAL remark, surprisingly – the 'hath' seems to be a modern embellishment. Although the concept is an ancient one, something close to the current wording first appears in the seventeenth century, in a play called *The Mourning Bride* by William Congreve:

Heaven has no rage, like love to hatred turn'd,
Nor Hell a fury like a woman scorn'd.

The interesting thing is that these words are spoken by Zara, the 'woman scorn'd' herself. So before we all get up in arms about the sexism of the seventeenth century, we should look at the original context: what Zara is saying is, 'No one dumps me and gets away with it – I'll show you.' Which makes it not much of a proverb, frankly.

The Mourning Bride is also the source of 'Music has charms to soothe a savage breast', which means it contains a lot of famous lines for a play you've never heard of. Congreve was only twenty-seven when he wrote it, and he never produced another tragedy – presumably having used up his store of maxims in this first attempt. Fools rush in...?

He who **hesitates** *is lost/ Better safe than sorry*

LOOK BEFORE YOU leap? Strike while the iron is hot? To risk it or to do a risk assessment first? This is the area in which the people who wrote proverbs seem to have had the most differences of opinion and having ended up copping out somewhat, leaving you to make up your own mind. So whether you opt for bravery or cowardice (or foolhardiness or prudence, if you prefer), you can be secure in the knowledge that you have a proverb to back you up.

Home *is where the heart is/ There's no place like home*

ONE DAY I shall write a book without quoting Tom Lehrer, but this isn't the one.

Lots of sentimental tosh has been written on the subject of home, much of it including the word 'humble', with the implication that however much you may travel, your affections lie with your homeland, home town, whatever it may be. 'East, west, home's best' is another version of the same thing, and of course Dorothy in *The Wizard of Oz* finally learned the lesson that there was no place like home, even if it was Kansas and in black and white to boot. An American songwriter called William Jerome caused quite a stir in 1901 when he wrote a song called 'Any Old Place I Can Hang my Hat Is Home Sweet Home to Me'; in 1962 Marvin Gaye followed this with 'Wherever I Lay my Hat (That's my Home)'. This wasn't what the 'Mom and apple pie' school of philosophy wanted at all.

Perhaps that's why the American public took Mr Lehrer's account of his home town so much to heart: for the sort of pure nostalgia that has you reaching for your handkerchief to wipe away a silent tear, it is hard to beat a place where the mayor's son is an arsonist, the maths teacher sells dirty pictures after school and Dan who runs the drug store kills his mother-in-law, grinds her up and sprinkles her remains over banana splits. In another song, his paean to the Deep South, 'I Wanna Go Back to Dixie', Lehrer also refers to his 'dear old Mammy': 'her cooking's lousy and her hands are clammy, but what the hell, it's home.'

Which, as so often with Tom Lehrer, says it all.

Honesty *is the best policy*

FIRST RECORDED IN 1599, this is a proverb open to at least

two interpretations: it could mean that honesty is the best policy simply because it is a Good Thing; or that honesty is politic, the course of action that is most likely to produce results. The first, of course, has the advantage of being on the moral high ground (*see* 'Virtue is its own reward'), but it does depend for its effectiveness on other people being honest too. The second was neatly summed up by Jerome K. Jerome in his periodical *The Idler*: 'It is always the best policy to speak the truth – unless, of course, you're an exceptionally good liar.'

If you're not sure which of these to choose, here's an 'apophthegm' by Richard Whately, a nineteenth-century Anglican archbishop of Dublin: 'Honesty is the best policy; but he who is governed by that maxim is not an honest man.' Discuss.[23]

There is **honour** among thieves

SINCE EVEN THE devil is said to look after his own (*see* page 70), it should come as no surprise that various subsets of society should also be loyal to each other. 'Thieves are never rogues among themselves,' pops up in *Don Quixote*, which was later turned into the musical *Man of La Mancha*. Pursuing the musical theme, in *Oliver!*

---

23 An apophthegm, by the way, is a short, clever saying expressing a general truth, based on a Greek word meaning 'to speak frankly'. So now you know.

Fagin, sending his boys out to pick a pocket or two, asks them to be back soon because he will worry about them while they're gone. And, still with *Oliver!*, Bill Sikes – firmly looking after number one and murdering his own girlfriend because she doesn't do precisely what he says – can be seen as the exception that proves the rule.

Hope *springs eternal in the human breast*

THIS IS ANOTHER quote from Alexander Pope (see 'To err is human' and 'A little learning is a dangerous thing') – this time from his *Essay on Man*. The line which follows it clarifies what he means, particularly if you note his use of capital letters:

Man never Is but always To Be blest.

In other words, we aren't actually blessed, we just expect to be: it is human nature to look on the bright side. Which is good news for anyone contemplating crossing their bridges before they come to them.

You can take a **horse** to water but you can't make it drink

OR, AS DOROTHY Parker once said, 'You can lead a whore to culture, but you can't make her think.'[24] Mrs Parker, a nonpareil among bitches, was at her best when laying into other women: her review of a book by Margot Asquith remarks that 'the affair between Margot Asquith and Margot Asquith will live as one of the prettiest love stories in all literature' and when the author wonders whimsically whether her choice of title for the book – *Lay Sermons* – is 'altogether happy', Dorothy's response is: 'Happier I think it would have been if, instead of the word "Sermons" she had selected the word "Off".'

But I digress. The point, which dates back to the twelfth century, is that there is only so much you can do to help anyone on the way to anything. Once they get there, they have to do the drinking – or the thinking – for themselves.

24 Tradition has it that she was challenged to use the word 'horticulture' in a sentence, though no tradition that I can find records why.

Hunger *is the best sauce*

OR, AS THE Roman philosopher Cicero observed, *Cibi condimentun esse famen* – that's 'Hunger is the spice of food' to you and me.

Not only is hunger the best sauce, it's the *healthiest* sauce. All the diet and nutrition gurus say that you should eat when you're hungry, not just because it is mealtime. The good news is that getting too hungry is bad for you, so you should have lots of little meals and healthy snacks throughout the day (but check out 'Enough is as good as a feast', before you get too excited).

Where **ignorance** *is bliss, 'tis folly to be wise*

ALTHOUGH THE CONCEPT of this proverb has been around since ancient times, Thomas Gray (of 'Elegy' fame) gave us the modern wording in a 1742 poem called 'Ode on a Distant Prospect of Eton College':

Thought would destroy their paradise.
No more; where ignorance is bliss,
'Tis folly to be wise.

The suggestion is that youthful innocence and ignorance

are highly enjoyable, while knowledge (and leaving Eton to go out into the world) brings care.

The idea persisted well into the twentieth century: in the late 1940s and early 1950s there was a BBC radio quiz programme called *Ignorance Is Bliss*, which asked questions along the lines of 'How many small persons feature in the fairy tale *Snow White and the Seven Dwarfs*?' or 'Who wrote Shakespeare's *Hamlet*?' It was extremely silly, but in those days everyone knew the questions were a joke – could you be so sure nowadays? When you read what are claimed to be genuine extracts from exam papers suggesting that some sixteen-year-olds believe the Pyramids are a range of mountains between France and Spain, or that Joan of Arc was Noah's sister, don't you wonder whether perhaps we have taken the cult of ignorance too far? *The Times* would agree. In November 2001, it drily observed: 'And the moral of our present situation is: if ignorance is bliss, why aren't more people happy?'

It's an **ill** wind that blows no one any good

MEANING THAT SOMETHING has to be really *really* bad for absolutely no one to benefit from it, this was quoted by Heywood in his *Dialogue of Proverbs* as long ago as 1546. So, for example, Milton, after an unhappy first marriage, was able to build a considerable reputation as an author of pamphlets on divorce. Various former British Cabinet ministers, having lost their seats in Parliament, have gone on to present TV documentaries or football programmes on the radio. There's hope for us all.

Imitation *is the sincerest form of flattery*

THIS ORIGINATES IN a book of aphorisms by Charles Caleb Colton, an English cleric of the early nineteenth century, well known, according to Wikipedia, for his eccentricities, which seem to have included wine collecting, gambling and being erratic about his duties as a vicar. He also came up with gems such as 'Corruption is like a ball of snow, once it's set a–rolling it must increase', 'Many speak the truth when they say that they despise riches, but they mean the riches possessed by others' and 'Silence is foolish if we are wise, but wise if we are foolish'.

In his preface, Colton reflects on the fact that many people write dull books, because dullness is limitless and unflagging: 'Horses may ride over her, and mules and asses may trample upon her, but, with an exhaustless and patient perversity, she continues her narcotic operations even to the end.' Wonderful stuff – why does no one read him any more?

Oh, yes, we were supposed to be talking about the proverb, weren't we? Well, the point is that if you bestir yourself to imitate someone your actions are probably speaking louder than your words and you may even be doing something useful, like buttering a few parsnips (*see* page 24).

Jack *of all trades is master of none*

THIS WAS RECORDED in the late sixteenth century and means that if you fritter your attention away on doing bits of this and bits of that, you may be competent but you won't excel at anything. According to the massively successful book *Outliers* by Malcolm Gladwell, practising your chosen craft/trade/skill for 10,000 hours over a period of ten years (that's about three hours a day, every day) makes the difference between success and failure – assuming a certain amount of innate talent. Gladwell cites sports stars such as the Williams sisters and Jonny Wilkinson, violinists who start playing at the age of four, and Bill Gates, whose schoolboy geekiness helped turned him into a quadzillionaire. People with this sort of dedication effectively make their own luck (*see* 'God helps those who help themselves').

Polymaths such as Stephen Fry and Simon Schama, who seem to be able to turn their hand successfully to everything and leave the rest of us boggling in admiration, come under the heading of the exception that proves the rule (*see* page 85).

If a **job's** worth doing, it's worth doing well

THIS IS ANOTHER pompous proverb, originating in a letter from Lord Chesterfield written in 1746 and now used only by smartarses. Yes, of course you should do things properly – the Welsh also point out that 'A work ill done must be twice done' – but modern management theory thinks highly of delegation, so you could always get someone else to do them for you (*see* 'Procrastination is the thief of time').

Never **judge** a book by its cover

SADLY IN THE book trade this is a complete no-no: everyone judges a book by its cover, and if you don't like the cover you aren't going to bother to pick it up and find out if the insides are any good. All that glitters may indeed not be gold but anything that glitters is still going to catch the eye. A twentieth-century expression, this is as true of people as it is of books; there is a world of truth in the sorrowful dictum of the late Sir John Mortimer that 'no power on earth ... can abolish the merciless class distinction between those who are physically desirable and the lonely, pallid, spotted, silent, unfancied majority'.

Knowledge *is power*

BACK TO THE Bible,[25] where the book of Proverbs points out that wisdom, understanding and knowledge are more powerful than evil or mischief, even if the evil and mischievous people don't play by the rules. Bizarrely, it goes on to say that one of the things that knowledge teaches you is to eat honey, because it is good, but if you were brought up on *Winnie the Pooh* you know this already.

On a more practical note, anyone who has knowledge of how to put up a bookshelf, stop the kitchen tap dripping and avoid the computer crashing just when I've forgotten to save something would wield great power in my house and is welcome to send me a business card.

But there's a dilemma here: if knowledge is power, what about ignorance being bliss? Power or happiness? The choice is yours.

It's the **last** *straw that breaks a camel's back*

WHEN PEOPLE FIND something after an exhaustive search, they often say – in all seriousness – 'It's always in the last

25 The dictionaries of quotations attribute 'Knowledge itself is power' to Francis Bacon, but he meant God's knowledge and power, which is not what we are talking about here.

place you look, isn't it?' Of course it is, I want to say: you stop looking after you've found it.

For pure silliness, 'It's the last straw that breaks a camel's back' isn't quite in this league, but it's close. Once the camel's back is broken, you're going to stop loading it, aren't you?

There is a 1655 variant suggesting that it is the horse's back that will break or that it is a feather that will do the breaking; an equivalent expression in French says that a pitcher carried too often to the well will finally break. All stating the obvious, you would think, but there is a grain of a message in amongst all this chaff: the tiniest little thing may tip someone over the edge if they are close enough to it, so don't push your luck.

Laugh *and the world laughs with you*

…weep and you weep alone;
For this stolid old earth
Has need of your mirth,
It has troubles enough of its own.

SO WROTE THE prolific American poet Ella Wheeler Wilcox in the early years of the twentieth century. This improving work was so popular as a music-hall monologue that 'Don't you Ella Wheeler Wilcox me' became a colloquialism for

'Don't preach at me'. She's more or less forgotten, now, poor woman, but she wasn't a barrel of laughs even in her prime.

Not only that, but this is another example of the proverb-makers contradicting themselves, because they also maintain that 'Misery loves company'. But I think the point is that if *you* are miserable, you want to share your misery with others; Ella was suggesting that those others may not be so keen to listen to you.

He who **laughs** last laughs longest

A MODERN EQUIVALENT of 'He laughs best who laughs last,' like a lot of proverbs, this can be interpreted in more than one way: either there's an element of getting your own back on someone who has played a trick on you (*see* 'Revenge is sweet'), or of biding your time to see if an investment (not necessarily financial) pays off. In either sense, it's a bit smug.

Laughter *is the best medicine*

THIS IDEA IS an ancient one, and is found in – appropriately – the book of Proverbs: 'A merry heart doeth good like a medicine: but a broken spirit drieth the bones'. It has prompted a surprising amount of research, with the result that some scientists claim that laughter has the same benefits as a mild workout – it stretches muscles, sends more oxygen to the tissues and generally makes you feel healthier. One study even suggests that laughing heartily for 10–15 minutes burns fifty calories.

But let's pause for thought here. The world may laugh with you over a joke or a re-run of *Fawlty Towers*; if you make a habit of laughing heartily for 10–15 minutes for no apparent reason, the world is going to think you are very strange indeed and cross the street to avoid you. It may be worth striving for a happy medium.

Least *said soonest mended*

THIS EXPRESSION, FIRST recorded *c*.1460, proffers the same idea as 'It's no use crying over spilt milk'. It is usually said by a third party trying to avert what promises to be an embarrassing family row.

A **leopard** *cannot change his spots*

NOT ONLY THAT, but he has a pattern of spots on his muzzle that remains constant throughout his life and is the most reliable way of identifying an individual: the leopard equivalent of fingerprints.

The origin of the proverb is the biblical book of Jeremiah, where it takes the form 'Can the Ethiopian change his skin, or the leopard his spots?' Without pausing to allow his audience to say, 'Um, well, no, I guess not', Jeremiah goes on: 'Then may ye also do good, that are accustomed to do evil.' He's ranting to the people of Jerusalem about how bad they are: 'I have seen thine adulteries, and thy neighings, the lewdness of thy whoredom, and thine abominations on the hills in the fields.'

Neighings? Abominations on the hills in the fields? If anyone has this on DVD, I'd be intrigued to see it.

More recently, Harry S. Truman, Democrat US President at the end of World War II and a man who often used proverbs to get his point across, had this to say about the opposition:

But it is important for the people of this country to recognize that time has not changed the fundamental outlook of the Republican Party since it was last in power. The leopard has not changed his spots; he has merely hired some public relations experts. They taught him to wear sheep's clothing, and to pour sweet nothings about unity in a soothing voice. But it's the same old leopard.

Which goes to show that politics – like leopards – haven't changed much over the last fifty years.

Lightning *never strikes twice in the same place*

A FIGURATIVE EXPRESSION meaning that the same disaster does not befall a person twice, based on an ancient literal belief that is now known to be wrong. Lightning *can* strike the same place more than once – indeed, it strikes the Empire State Building about a hundred times a year without doing much damage, because it tends to hit the twenty-two-storey-high lightning rod/television aerial attached to the top of the building.

But there's another interpretation of this saying, as the American writer Percival Wilde put forward in 1942 in the following piece of dialogue from *Tinsley's Bones*:

The Witness: They say that lightning never strikes twice in the same place.
Mr Blodgett: It don't because the second time the place ain't there.

Obvious, really.

A **little** learning is a dangerous thing

A little Learning is a dangerous Thing;
Drink deep, or taste not the Pierian Spring:
There shallow Draughts intoxicate the Brain,
And drinking largely sobers us again.

THIS IS POPE'S *Essay on Criticism* again (*see* 'To err is human, to forgive divine'). The Pierian Spring was sacred to the Muses, so it means a source of inspiration. The point is that it is all too easy to look something up on the Internet and overexcitedly assume you know everything there is to know; when you read a bit more on the subject you discover that there is rather more to it than that. So, particularly in this Wiki-oriented age, there is a salutary lesson here.

Little things please little minds

YOU MAY THINK this is just something your mother used to say in one of her more sarcastic moods, but in fact its origins are classical: Ovid's *Ars Amatoria* again (*see* 'The grass is always greener on the other side of the fence'). This time the poet is warning the man bent on seduction to be on his guard if he takes a lady to watch a chariot race – somebody nudging her from the row behind may be quite enough to distract her attention: 'The merest trifle is enough to win these butterfly ladies. Why, hosts of men have succeeded with a woman merely by the attentive manner in which they have arranged a cushion for her, or fanned her with a fan, or put a stool beneath her dainty feet.'[26]

The first part of this is often translated 'Small things enthral light minds', but the word 'butterfly' makes the meaning even clearer − women are being depicted as utterly frivolous. But, as I mentioned before, Ovid's poem upset a lot of people (not least the entire female sex, I should imagine), so perhaps we should be careful about taking what he says as gospel.

Nowadays few people remember the sexual provenance of this expression and are content to use it to describe such things as grown-ups playing childish games or mice running round and round in wheels (*see* 'When the cat's away the mice will play').

Live *and let live*

A MANTRA FOR tolerance that we should all observe. As a proverb it's hundreds of years old, is found in various languages throughout Europe, was used to promote truces

---

26 I realize that taking a lady to a chariot race and putting a stool beneath her feet may not be something you do very often, but in modern parlance taking her anywhere she is likely to be chatted up by someone sitting nearby would be running the same risk, as far as Ovid was concerned.

over Christmas during World War I, and yet look what a bigoted, intolerant, dogmatic mess the world is in.

That's all I'm going to say, because I promised myself I would get through this entry without mentioning James Bond and I'll get a quantum of solace out of the fact that I've done it.

Oh no! I blew it. But at least it was for your eyes only.

The **longest** journey begins with a single step

ATTRIBUTED TO LAO-TZU, the founder of Taoism, who – like Confucius – was a great soundbite man. I particularly like 'Governing a large country is like frying a fish. You spoil it with too much poking' and 'Wise men don't need to prove their point; men who need to prove their point aren't wise'. But this is perhaps his most famous line, and certainly one of his best. So, according to Lao-Tzu, it doesn't matter whether you are looking before you leap or rushing in where angels fear to tread – you just have to make a start somewhere.

Don't **look** a gift horse in the mouth

DATING BACK TO the time of Saint Jerome, this expression is based on the idea that looking in a horse's mouth is a way of estimating its age, assuming you know how to assess the quality of a horse's teeth (a dying art where I live, I'm ashamed to say). And the point is that this is ungracious when someone is making you a present of a horse. So when someone gives you something you don't want, remember your manners (*see* 'Manners makyth man'), say thank you as if you mean it and display the gift prominently on the mantelpiece next time they come to visit. Then – and only then – is it acceptable to take it to the charity shop.

Look before you leap

OR, AS THE proverb ran back in 1350: 'First loke and aftirward lepe'. There's a lot in this book about prudence versus courage (*see* 'Fools rush in when angels fear to tread' and 'Nothing ventured, nothing gained') and this saying comes down on the side of prudence. It's the moral in a fable by Aesop about a fox who falls into a well and persuades a thirsty goat to jump in after him, enabling the fox to escape but leaving the goat stranded. If you think you are brighter than the average goat, you may not feel that you have to take this too much to heart.

What you **lose** *on the swings you gain on the roundabouts*

SOME PEOPLE PHRASE this the other way round – putting the gaining first – so this is a bit like the discussion of whether the calm comes before or after the storm (*see* page 49). But what it boils down to is that what goes around comes around and that it will all even itself out in the end.

Love *is blind*

See 'Beauty is in the eye of the beholder', page 33.

Every **man** *has his price*

WHEN YOU HEAR of the financial goings-on of politicians, bankers and the like, you do begin to wonder whether there is anyone left who has any principles when large sums of cash are involved. And, despite the wording of the proverb, which has its origins as far back as 100 AD, this applies to either sex.

Consider the old story about George Bernard Shaw meeting a beautiful young socialite at a party and putting forward the theory that everyone would do anything if the price were high enough.

She protested, and he asked, 'Would you sleep with me for a million pounds?'

She blushed and simpered and did all those things that young socialites do, like saying, 'I'm flattered, Mr Shaw.'

'Well,' he replied, 'would you do it for ten pounds?'

Abrupt change of mood on the part of the socialite: 'Mr Shaw! What do you take me for?'

'We've already established what you are,' said the great moralist. 'Now we are merely haggling over the price.'

If you've seen the film *Indecent Proposal*, in which Demi Moore slept with Robert Redford for $1 million, you'll probably agree that it's better just not to go there. I'm of the generation that would have paid good money to sleep with Robert Redford (in his Sundance Kid days), but let's not go there either.

A **man** is known by the company he keeps

MEANING THAT IF you hang about with layabouts, people

will assume you are a layabout too – which may well be true, but you need to decide whether that is what you want them to think. While it is generally OK for birds of a feather to flock together, this proverb takes an altogether more judgemental stance. Indeed, it was used as a moral maxim in the context of marriage in the sixteenth century.

A **man's** best friend is his dog

ONE OF THE many ways in which you can divide the world in two is to split them into dog people and cat people. Cat people admire the way that a cat will show you affection when and if it wants to, but will otherwise be anything from casually aloof to plain dismissive. They cite this as evidence of an intelligent and independent nature.

By contrast, a dog that you have never met before will greet you as a long-lost friend, knock over coffee tables with the enthusiasm of its tail-wagging and generally make you feel you are the most important person in the world, which is just fine with me.

But never mind cats – are dogs better friends than people? Well, when was the last time a dog:

• argued about what to watch on TV or whose turn it was to drive home?

- was half an hour (or indeed half a minute) late for dinner and turned up smashed?

- told your boss something you'd discussed in the strictest confidence?

- took offence because you said that new dress made it look fat?

I rest my case.

One **man's** meat is another man's poison

A VARIATION ON 'There's no accounting for taste' (*see* 'Beauty is in the eye of the beholder'). The source is the Roman poet Lucretius, who wrote a long poem 'On the Nature of Things' in which he wonders why:

what is food to one to some becomes
Fierce poison, as a certain snake there is
Which, touched by spittle of a man, will waste
And end itself by gnawing up its coil.
Again, fierce poison is the hellebore
To us, but puts the fat on goats and quails.

Goats and quails? Where did he see goats and quails eating hellebores? Perhaps in the same place he saw a man spitting

125

on a (presumably live) snake, which suggests that he is living in an age before anyone had thought of discretion being the better part of valour.

Manners *makyth man*

WHEN I WAS at school, there were 850 of us girls with only three men on the teaching staff; one of those men was called Mr Manners. He was young and good-looking and he had to teach history to groups of giggling adolescents in a room that had 'Manners Makyth Man' inscribed over the fireplace. (I promise I am not making this up.)

The poor man must have cursed William of Wykeham every time he walked into that classroom. William was the founder of New College Oxford and of Winchester College, and both these institutions have had 'Manners makyth man' as their motto since Day One, 1379 and Day One, 1382 respectively, William having been a stickler for good manners and for good behaviour generally.

A gossipy aside about William, though. He was bishop of Winchester at a time when the bishops had a palace on London's South Bank (the rose window is still there, between the replica of the *Golden Hind* and the Tate Modern). For 500 years – including the period of William's bishopric – the bishops were the only people allowed to license prostitutes in the area, and the girls became known as 'Winchester geese'. But I'm sure William was very polite to them.

So do manners make us? Well, I wouldn't go as far as that, but they can do no harm. Particularly when in Rome (*see* page 154).

Marry *in haste, repent at leisure*

THIS FIRST APPEARED in print in *The Old Batchelour*, the comedy of manners by William Congreve dating from 1693:

Thus grief still treads upon the heels of pleasure:
Married in haste, we may repent at leisure.

Even longer ago than that, Henry VIII is the obvious person to start with when thinking about ill-judged marriages: he would have done better if 'Thou shalt not marry thy brother's widow and then try to wriggle out of it on the spurious grounds that it was never legal in the first place' and 'Thou shalt not marry a woman of whom thou hast seen only a flattering portrait' had been in the Ten Commandments. When it came to wife number five, Catherine Howard – aged about twenty to his forty-nine – he both married in haste and repented in haste, but here perhaps the moral is 'There's no fool like an old fool'. Earlier he had pursued Anne Boleyn for a dogged eight years, but then he wasn't getting the sort of familiarity that enabled him to breed contempt, or indeed to breed anything else...

A **miss** is as good as a mile

DATING AS FAR back as 1614, this is perfectly true, once you have got to the bottom of what it means. Which is, 'If you miss, it doesn't matter if you've missed by a hair's breadth or by a mile (1.6 kilometres, if you're being literal about it) – you've still missed.' Hitting the post in football, sending the ball juddering round the pocket in snooker, flinging yourself across the tennis court and *just* failing to pick the ball up: it may be exciting for the spectators, but you still haven't scored.

Money doesn't grow on trees

THIS IS SCARCITY thinking, meaning that money isn't in plentiful supply, ready for plucking, like the leaves on a tree. But there is a plant called the money tree (*Pachira aquatica*) that is associated with good fortune and good feng shui and is often given as a present at Chinese New Year. Bizarrely, it originates in the swamps of South America, but was adopted as a bonsai plant in Taiwan in the 1980s. It has several stems braided together and is supposed to be lucky because of its five-lobed leaves; some of the leaves have seven lobes, which is luckier still. Normally to turn a tree into a bonsai specimen you prune its roots but also constantly trim its leaves; with the money tree the upper part of the plant is allowed to grow so that it produces lots of lucky foliage.

A completely different money tree (*Crassula ovata*, sometimes known as the jade plant) is also thought to be lucky, so grow it as a houseplant and watch those lottery winnings roll in. Or not.

Necessity *is the mother of invention*

SKIP FORWARD A few pages to 'Variety is the spice of life' and you'll find mention of William Cowper, who wrote a poem about a sofa. Here's a quote from the early part of it, before he felt he had exhausted the subject of furniture:

Thus first necessity invented stools,
Convenience next suggested elbow-chairs,
And luxury the accomplished sofa last.

The first line is the important one here: somebody got tired of standing up all the time, so he invented something to sit on. And so it has been throughout history: when somebody needed a cart to carry a heavier load than he could manage himself, he invented the wheel; when buildings got taller and people didn't want to walk up all those stairs, they invented the lift. It works with words, too: when somebody (and this isn't the place to argue over who it was) came up with a machine that enabled you to talk over long distances, they had to dream up the word 'telephone'.

In 1726, the eponymous hero of *Gulliver's Travels* by Jonathan Swift had to take the same 'needs must' (see below) approach: 'I soaled my Shoes with wood, which I cut from a Tree... No man could more verify the Truth... That Necessity is the Mother of Invention.'

The eighteenth-century French philosopher Voltaire took the idea one stage further when he wrote, 'If God did not exist, it would be necessary to invent him.' This is another quotation that is frequently taken out of context and, because Voltaire was passionately and vociferously anti-Christian, is great fun to argue over when you've had a few drinks; what he actually meant was more prosaic than it seems at first glance – that the fear of God, and the fear of punishment in the Afterlife, act as deterrents to criminals and thus help to maintain social order. According to one of my reference books, Voltaire's ideas were an important part of the intellectual climate that led to the French Revolution, which happened a mere eleven years after his death, so either he or God got something wrong somewhere.

Needs *must when the devil drives*

THIS ODD EXPRESSION makes a bit more sense if you go back to the original, 'He needs must go when the devil drives', and even more sense if you turn it into modern English. It then becomes something like 'When the devil is driving, you must go where he takes you'. Or you could loosely translate it as 'A man's gotta do what a man's gotta do'. The saying has its origins in medieval times, when people tended to have more respect for the Forces of Darkness than we do now. In the twenty-first century none of those headless coachmen you see in old horror films would ever pass their driving test.

No **news** *is good news/ Bad news travels fast*

HERE IS ANOTHER pairing of proverbs that say more or less the same thing ('If anything awful had happened, you'd have heard'), but in these days of constant communication good news travels fast too, as does news that isn't really news at all. Look at the complete trivia that people put on Facebook, and the instant responses they provoke, if you don't believe me.

So these are rare examples of proverbs that have been around since antiquity being rendered obsolete by technology.

Noblesse *oblige*

'WHY DO WE say it in French?' we asked under *Plus ça change, plus c'est la même chose* and yes, well spotted, we could easily ask the same question here. This time the answer is that 'Nobility brings its own obligations' sounds too up itself for words, and wouldn't fit comfortably on to a coat of arms.[27]

Although the concept of the nobility – or in America, the rich – helping the poor was propounded in France by the nineteenth-century novelist Honoré de Balzac, and in the States by the philanthropist Andrew Carnegie (he of the hall), it reached a much wider audience when it became the motto of the *Marvel* comic hero Spiderman. He expresses it as 'With great power comes great responsibility', but it means the same thing. Superheroes demand no praise, which is why Spiderman wears a mask and Clark Kent hides behind his glasses; they don't seek fame but offer help because it is the right thing to do. Good on them.

This expression shouldn't, by the way, be confused with *droit de seigneur*, which means that if you are lord of the manor you are entitled to shag the milkmaid. The fact that this attitude is no longer widely accepted is one of the (many) reasons why lords of the manor and milkmaids are rather thinner on the ground these days than they used to be.

27 I don't know that *Noblesse oblige* belongs on any coat of arms; it just sounds as if it ought to, like *Honi soit qui mal y pense* or *Sans peur et sans reproche*.

There's **nothing** new under the sun

THIS IS A quote from the Old Testament book of Ecclesiastes, in which someone known as the Preacher sets out his thesis that 'all is vanity' – one generation passes away and another comes to take its place; the sun rises and sets and rises again – so basically what *is* the point? There's a lot more to this effect, with great emphasis on vexation of the spirit and hating life. Surprisingly cynical for the Bible, you might think, but that's what it says.

Nowadays, of course, we have lots of new stuff that they didn't have in the Preacher's time. He says he gets no pleasure out of planting gardens and orchards and making pools of water to water them with, so maybe he would have been happier in the era of cosmetic surgery and Sky Plus.

Nothing ventured, nothing gained/ Faint heart never won fair lady/ Fortune favours the brave

THE ROMAN AUTHORS Terence and Virgil both said something along the lines of 'Fortune assists the brave', Terence talking about getting your own way in a love affair (winning fair lady, in fact) and Virgil putting the words into the mouth of a general urging his troops into battle. Nowadays most of us would just say, 'Go for it.'

You can't make an **omelette** without breaking eggs

UNDENIABLE: IT WOULD be unpleasantly crunchy if you did. This seems originally to have been a French expression; the Italians say the same thing but with pancakes rather than an omelette, and I have also seen a Russian equivalent attributed to Lenin, 'If you chop down a forest, splinters will fly.' Interestingly, some sources attribute the French version to Robespierre, one of the most influential figures of the French Revolution. Clearly the moral is that, whatever nationality you are, if you want a halfway decent revolution – or to have any chance of achieving a less violent goal – you have to take the rough with the smooth.

Out of sight, out of mind

See 'Absence makes the heart grow fonder', page 23.

Patience is a virtue

IN THE BEGINNING there were seven heavenly virtues, made up of three theological ones (faith, hope and charity) and four cardinal ones (fortitude, justice, temperance and prudence). Faith, hope and charity are laid out in Saint

Paul's first letter to the Corinthians as qualities that bring man closer to God; the cardinal virtues had been defined by Ancient Greek philosophers but were later adopted into the Christian Church as the foundation for a moral life.

No mention of patience, you'll notice. She came later, as one of the Seven Contrary Virtues – contrary, that is, to the Seven Deadly Sins, where each virtue is 'paired' with a sin and counterbalances it. Patience is said to be the virtue that will protect against the sin of anger; similarly humility helps you guard against pride, diligence against sloth and so on. The concept came from the *Psychomachia* or *Battle for the Soul*, an epic poem written by Prudentius in the fifth century AD. As an allegory of the struggle between good (Christian) virtues and bad (everyone else's) vices, it was immensely influential, so patience did belatedly gain credibility as a virtue.

That said, the saying is one of those annoying ones, like 'Children should be seen and not heard' and 'Cleanliness is next to godliness', that it is difficult to utter without looking and sounding immensely pleased with yourself.

He who **pays** the piper calls the tune

TAKE YOUR PICK: you could consider this a more poetic way of saying, 'Money talks' or a more grown-up way of saying, 'It's my ball and I'm going home'. Either way, if

135

you're paying the bills, you're in charge. The saying may
originate from the time when pipers used to play music
to amuse the guests at taverns or out on the green, and
expected to be paid for this entertainment; it makes sense
that the person who came up with the money could
choose what tunes the piper played – a bit like putting
coins in a jukebox.

Throughout history wise men (and it is mostly men)
have written about the importance of money: the Latin
poet Horace advised, 'If possible honestly, if not somehow,
make money'; Samuel Pepys mused, 'But it is pretty to
see what money will do'; and Somerset Maugham came
up with 'Money is like a sixth sense without which you
cannot make a complete use of the other five'. Even the
Bible, amazingly, says, 'Wine maketh merry, but money
answereth all things.' Cynical, maybe, but try calling the
tune without money and you're likely to get short shrift
from the average piper.

The **pen** is mightier than the sword

TO TURN THIS proverb into something with contemporary
relevance, you have to update it to 'the spread of information
is mightier than the bomb' and then it becomes quite an
interesting talking point.

The original sense was that anything written (and

promulgated, once the printing press arrived and literacy became more widespread) had the ability to influence many more people over a longer period of time than anything that could be achieved by mere warfare. The power of the written word and the ideas it can express is underlined by the regimes that have, throughout history, banned or burned books: the works of Darwin, the Bible, the Koran, anything written by a Jew in Nazi Germany and even, according to Wikipedia, *Black Beauty* (banned in South Africa in the days of apartheid because it had the word 'black' in the title) have all fallen foul of the censor or the bonfire at some time or another. And, of course, because news now zaps around the world in nanoseconds, 'spreading the word' is easier and more powerful than ever before.

The worrying thing, however, is that, since 1945, 'the sword' has become rather more powerful than it used to be and could equally wipe us all out in nanoseconds. On this subject, the Roman philosopher Cicero – *Cedant arma togae*, or 'Arms give way to persuasion' – came down on the side of words as, centuries later, did Churchill: 'It is better to jaw-jaw than to war-war.'

Take care of the **pennies** and the pounds will take care of themselves

In letters he wrote to his son in 1750, Lord Chesterfield said that this piece of advice came from the lips of William Lowndes, Secretary of the Treasury, presumably a recognized source of wisdom on the subject. Be warned, though – it's easy to sound holier-than-thou with this attitude and to get the reputation of being a tightwad. If you think of yourself as more of a 'big picture' person who doesn't like getting bogged down in details, the alternative expression 'Penny wise, pound foolish' may suit you better. (*See also* 'Every little helps' for more on the thrifty aspect of this proverb.)

In for a **penny**, in for a pound

Originally this referred to a financial commitment; now it has a much broader remit. W. S. Gilbert uses it – and four other proverbs – in a romantic context in a verse in *Iolanthe*, showing, by the way, just how thin the dividing line between proverb and cliché can be:

Faint heart never won fair lady!
Nothing venture, nothing win –
Blood is thick, but water's thin –
In for a penny, in for a pound –

It's Love that makes the world go round!

In modern parlance, the saying tends to mean 'Oh, what the hell, let's go for it' or, more positively, 'If a job's worth doing, it's worth doing well' (*see* page 112).

People *who live in glass houses shouldn't throw stones*

THE ITALIANS SAY, 'He that has a head of glass must not throw stones at another', which amounts to the same thing – be careful that you aren't criticizing someone for something of which you may be guilty yourself.[28]

There is, however, a thing called tempered glass, which has a surface compression of 10,000 psi (as opposed to 3,500 for ordinary annealed glass) and it resists breakage by small missiles travelling approximately twice as fast as things that would break general-purpose glass. It's used in all sorts of stuff from squash courts to the rear windows of cars. So if you want to live in a glass house and still get away with throwing stones, that's the type to go for.

28 If you do, you may be accused of being a pot calling a kettle black.

Little **pitchers** have big ears

NOT QUITE AS silly as walls (*see* page 179), because in fact some small jugs do have large ear-shaped handles. But this isn't intended to be taken literally; it means, 'Be careful what you say in front of the children.' However small they may be, the principle is the same: they will be earwigging – and asking you embarrassing questions about what a boob job is and all sorts of other things you'd rather they hadn't overheard.

Possession is nine points of the law

SOME SAY NINE-TENTHS, but it amounts to the same thing. It's a more grown-up way of mouthing the smug childhood jibe, 'Finders keepers, losers weepers.' Think squatter's rights (or adverse possession, if you prefer a more technical term): stay in a place long enough and you could end up having the right to be there; in the meantime you can thumb your nose at the owner and say, 'So what are you going to do about it?'

Practice makes perfect

A LATIN PROVERB, this is a little on the optimistic side, I feel: practice makes better, certainly, but no amount of practice is going to make my piano playing better than adequate. On the other hand, I have no chance of getting any better if I *don't* practise – and that is the point. Studying something in theory is all very well; putting it into practice is the only way to find out if it works or if you have got the hang of it. As another less familiar proverb has it, 'An ounce of practice is worth a pound of precept.' (For those of you who have gone metric, this means that practice is sixteen times more valuable than precept, but I'm not sure that anyone has worked it out precisely.)

In the UK even nature, it seems, follows this maxim, as reported in 2002 in *Country Life* magazine: 'The quality of the [blackbird's] song improves as the season progresses … This, presumably, is a matter of practice makes perfect.' There is also encouragement to be taken from the South African golfer Gary Player who, on being congratulated once on a lucky shot, is supposed to have replied, 'The more I practise, the luckier I get.'

Prevention *is better than cure*

THIS IS ONE of those statements that is so self-evident you wonder how it ever attained the status of a proverb. But you don't have to go back very far in the history of medicine to realize that it wasn't always so. For centuries the devil was blamed for serious illnesses and misfortunes, and there wasn't much anyone could do about that. It was only in the mid-nineteenth century that Louis Pasteur discovered that if you inoculated people against rabies they stopped getting rabies; Joseph Lister realized that if you put antiseptic on wounds people stopped dying of infections; and the obstetrician Ignaz Semmelweis speculated that if his students washed their hands in a solution of chlorinated lime before delivering babies, fewer women would contract puerperal fever. Around the same time it also occurred to some bright spark that the incidence of cholera was lower in areas where the drains were covered. And if you have seen the film *Brief Encounter*,[29] you may remember that Trevor Howard's character was a passionate advocate of preventive medicine, particularly with respect to coal miners' lungs. This seemed very exciting and innovative as late as 1945 (or it did to Celia Johnson, anyway, but she had gone a bit misty-eyed by this time).

So it is quite surprising to find that the proverb dates back at least to the seventeenth century, when a clergyman called Thomas Adams (whom we shall meet again under 'The road to Hell is paved with good intentions') wrote, 'Prevention is so much better than healing, because it saves the labour of being sick.'

The idea need not be restricted to health and medicine – in a broader sense is means much the same as 'A stitch in time saves nine' (*see* page 165).

29 As I do hope you have.

Pride *goes (or comes) before a fall*

THE GREEKS HAD a word for this, hubris, which means precisely the sort of pride that does go before a fall. It was used specifically with reference to the classical theatre, to describe the 'tragic flaw' in a hero's character that brought about his downfall – ambition in Macbeth, jealousy in Othello, wasting time talking about hawks and handsaws in Hamlet,[30] that sort of thing. I am aware that none of these comes from a Greek tragedy, but if I start discussing the characters of Oedipus and Orestes and Agamemnon you'll think I am showing off, which would be a sort of hubris in itself.

Procrastination *is the thief of time/ Never put off until tomorrow what you can do today*

THE FORMER IS a posh way of saying the latter, because if you put something off until tomorrow and tomorrow and tomorrow (which is all that 'procrastination' means – *cras* is the Latin for 'tomorrow') you will sooner or later find you have run out of time. In *David Copperfield*, Dickens gives us two for the price of one by using both proverbs in the same sentence: 'Never do to-morrow what you can do to-day. Procrastination is the thief of time.' Abraham

---

30 Did you miss him? It's been a while since he got a name check.

Lincoln (who was a bit of a Goody Two-Shoes, when all is said and done) was in favour of these maxims too: 'Whatever piece of business you have in hand,' he wrote, 'before stopping, do all the labour pertaining to it which can then be done.'

As ever, the moralizers have to stand up against the cynics, who maintain 'Never do today what you can put off till tomorrow' or 'Never put off till tomorrow what you can get someone else to do for you today'. But before you write this off as pure idleness, check out 'If a job's worth doing, it's worth doing well' (*see* page 112).

There are a number of good quotes about idleness, though, my favourites being Jerome K. Jerome's *Idle Thoughts of an Idle Fellow*, 'It is impossible to enjoy idling thoroughly unless one has plenty of work to do'; and the line attributed to the Regency dandy Beau Brummell that 'whether it was summer or winter, he always liked to have the morning well-aired before he got up'.

The **proof** of the pudding is in the eating

THE ORIGIN OF the phrase in this form dates back to the early 1600s and is another of the 'appearances can be deceptive' school (*see* 'All that glitters is not gold' and 'Never judge a book by its cover'). If you subscribe to the view that there is no such thing as a bad pudding, particularly if it has chocolate in it, then obviously you will want to prove (in the sense of 'testing the goodness of', *see* 'The exception proves the rule') any pudding you come across. Possibly twice, just to be sure.

A **prophet** is without honour in his own country

According to Matthew in the New Testament, 'A prophet is not without honour, save in his own country, and in his own house.' As a follower of Christ, Matthew would have known what he was talking about – no doubt the people of Nazareth went around saying, 'That's Joseph the carpenter's boy. I remember him when he was a snotty-nosed kid – what's he doing calling himself the Messiah?' And they would certainly have said 'him' and 'he' rather than 'Him' and 'He'. 'No man is a hero to his valet' – attributed to Madame Anne Bigot du Cornuel (1605–95) – means much the same thing. In the same vein, an even earlier observation comes from Antigonus Gonatus (*c.*312–239 BC), the Macedonian king who refuted the suggestion that he might be a god by replying, 'The man who carries my chamberpot knows better.'

In other words, snotty nose, toilet habits or whatever – if people know you too well, you're not going to kid them

145

that you can do a nifty trick with loaves and fishes or that you are in any way divine.

Punctuality *is the politeness of kings*

THIS SAYING IS attributed to King Louis XVIII of France, though he said it in French: *L'exactitude est la politesse des rois.* Presumably he thought that punctuality was the preserve of royalty and not a trait found in the common man (or woman) – or maybe he meant that if you were punctual you were behaving *like* a king. Whatever; punctuality is the politeness of everyone, in my view. Expecting people to hang around waiting for you because you think your time is more important than theirs is downright rude.

Never **put** *off until tomorrow what you can do today*

See 'Procrastination is the thief of time', page 144

You can't fit a **quart** *into a pint pot*

PERHAPS THE MOST annoying proverb in the whole book, likely to be uttered by someone who has just watched you struggling to make your clothes fit into a suitcase that is too small for them (or your stomach into a pair of jeans, ditto). It's been around since at least the nineteenth century and was probably annoying even then.

A quart (a liquid measure of about 3.5 litres) is equal to 2 pints. Note the word 'liquid' here: it's crucial. You can't squash liquid the way you can squash clothes into a suitcase to make them fit. So you can't fit a quart into a pint pot. Watch my lips. The pint pot is too small. The liquid will spill all over the place. Don't even think about it.

It never **rains** but it pours

FIRST OF ALL you have to understand this old-fashioned use of the word 'but'. Nowadays we might say, 'It never rains unless it pours' or 'It never rains without pouring', but as with so many proverbs, if you rephrase it so that it makes sense it doesn't sound nearly as good. Even so, it isn't true if you take it literally: I am looking out my window as I write and it is definitely raining, but in a haphazard, drizzly, can't-make-its-mind-up sort of way – by no stretch of the imagination pouring.

So let's not take it literally. The point is that, as Shakespeare puts it, sorrows come 'not single spies but in battalions'. That's from *Hamlet*,[31] and it's what the king says when

31 And here he is again.

Ophelia goes mad after her father has died and Hamlet has been exiled and I dare say Elsinore Rovers are about to be relegated. Lots of people maintain that accidents or disasters come in threes, which is less gloomy than battalions but still a feeble excuse for dropping a plate on the kitchen floor after you have knocked over a glass of wine and trodden in the dog's water bowl. Why not just go to bed and sleep it off?

Revenge is sweet/Revenge is a dish best served (or eaten) cold

As YOU CAN imagine, revenge has been a rich source of material for the creators of soundbites over the centuries. Bons mots on the subject include the virtuous 'An eye for an eye makes the whole world blind', which I have seen attributed both to Mahatma Gandhi and to Martin Luther King; the philosophical 'A man that studieth revenge keeps his own wounds green, which otherwise would heal and do well' (Francis Bacon); and 'If an injury has to be done to a man it should be so severe that his vengeance need not be feared', from the ever-practical Machiavelli.

There is no question of forgiving and forgetting with either of these proverbs. The only debate is whether a quick revenge – 'He hit me so I hit him back' – is sweet enough, or whether something lingering is more satisfying. In the old Ealing comedy *Kind Hearts and Coronets*, Dennis

Price's character took the longer term view: killing off eight relatives who stand between you and a dukedom because the current duke was unkind to your mother twenty years ago is a fine example of serving your revenge well chilled. (*See also* 'He who laughs last laughs longest').

As to the origins of the saying, the film *Star Trek II: The Wrath of Khan* quotes 'Revenge is a dish best served cold' as an old Klingon proverb and I'll upset a lot of people if I suggest otherwise.

The **road** to hell is paved with good intentions

MEANING 'GOOD INTENTIONS aren't enough; in fact, good intentions are no good at all unless you carry them out', the expression is often attributed to Dr Johnson, but it is a lot older than that. It can be traced back to a twelfth-century Cistercian monk called Bernard of Clairvaux (later Saint Bernard, but nothing to do with the dog of the same name), who put it succinctly: 'Hell is full of good intentions or desires.' Later (but still a hundred years before Johnson), a seventeenth-century cleric called Thomas Adams developed the theme:

I know there are many that intend much, but do nothing; and that earth is full of good purposes, but heaven only full of good works; and that the tree gloriously leaved with intentions, without fruit, was cursed; and that a lewd heart may be so far smitten and convinced at a sermon, as to will a forsaking of some sin. Which thoughts are but swimming notions, and vanishing motions; embryons [sic]*, or abortive births.*

In other words, the moment you get out of church and the sermon is no longer ringing in your ears, you go back to your bad old ways. *And that won't do.*

Another pearl of wisdom from Thomas Adams was 'Prevention is better than cure' (*see* page 142).

All **roads** lead to Rome

A MEDIEVAL PHRASE, used by Chaucer, this was more or less true in the days when Rome was the centre of the ancient world, with all roads in its empire radiating back to the capital city. Nowadays if you're in France you'll find all roads lead to Paris, in England to London and in the USA the distances are so vast that it's better to fly. What the saying means is that different methods can produce the same goal – as long as you offset your carbon footprint.

A **rolling** stone gathers no moss

IN THE EARLY days of this proverb's life, stability was seen as a virtue and a rolling stone was to be pitied – it didn't gather possessions or emotional ties. In his *Adages*, the Renaissance scholar Erasmus wrote (in Greek and Latin, of course), 'A rolling stone does not gather sea-weed' and 'A rolling stone is not covered with moss'. In the 1573 edition of his long instructional poem, *Five Hundred Points of Good Husbandrie*, Thomas Tusser took time out from farming to expand on the theme:

The stone that is rolling can gather no moss,
For master and servant oft changing is loss.

By the 1960s, though, people had become confused. Bob Dylan rhymed 'rolling stone' with 'complete unknown', addressing a girl who had started life wealthy and privileged but was now living on the streets – so for her being a rolling stone was a real comedown. But in the same year, the Rolling Stones had three Number One hits,[32] so to the young at least a rolling stone must have seemed pretty darned glamorous and gathering moss was something boring that your parents did.

Then in 1972, Motown group The Temptations reached Number One with a song about another 'rolling stone' – in this case the singer's no-good Papa. Wherever that

---

32 1965, 'The Last Time', 'Satisfaction' and 'Get off of my Cloud'. Five bonus points if you got them all.

gentleman laid his hat was his home and when he died, according to the refrain, 'All he left us was alone.'

So this is an example of a proverb whose meaning has evolved over the years. Is home where the heart is, or is any old place you can find to hang your hat home sweet home to you? Your call.

Rome *wasn't built in a day*

NO, BUT IT would have been finished a lot more quickly if Remus hadn't made a tactless remark that caused Romulus to take time out from building to murder him. It's one of several proverbs that hark back 2,000 years to the days when Rome was the hub of a mighty empire.

You've probably seen the postcard/mouse mat/fridge magnet that says, 'The impossible we do at once. Miracles take a little longer.' Well, that is the message of this saying: you can't get great results at the drop of a hat, and there is no point in panicking, bullying or otherwise chivvying your underlings to achieve the unachievable. Even if you are the boss.

When in **Rome**, do as the Romans do

THIS ISN'T SO much a proverb as a piece of basic courtesy: it's only polite to follow local customs. I have to confess that even in Rome I find it easier to be polite once I have had a decent cup of tea in the morning, but I don't insist on porridge or kippers. *That* would be rude.

Funnily enough, the origin of this proverb is also connected with food. Saint Monica and her son Saint Augustine, faced with a dilemma, asked Saint Ambrose: 'At Rome they fast on Saturday, but not so at Milan; which practice ought to be observed?' Unphased, Ambrose replied: 'When I am at Milan, I do as they do at Milan; but when I go to Rome…' I'll leave it to you to guess the rest.

What's **sauce** for the goose is sauce for the gander

IN A CULINARY sense I'm sure this is true: it may be that top chefs prefer one gender of goose over the other for texture or succulence, but I've never heard it said that you should serve sage and onion with the one and apples with the other. In the metaphorical sense of 'what is suitable for a man is suitable for a woman', it is more debatable, as it's another of those proverbs that seem to justify bad behaviour (*see* 'All's fair in love and war'), usually in a sexual sense: 'He's been unfaithful to me, so why shouldn't I be unfaithful to him?' If this is the way you want to run your life, who am I to argue? On the other hand, it may result in your cooking your goose, which might not be such a good idea.

On the subject of geese, *Brewer's Dictionary of Phrase and Fable* is full of good stuff which has sadly fallen from the language. The 'goose month', for example, used to be the month of a woman's 'lying-in' after giving birth, which gave rise to the 'gander month', a time when the husband was likely to be at a loose end and go out gallivanting. When the cat's away, eh?

The best laid **schemes** o' mice an' men gang aft a-gley

THIS IS A quote from Robert Burns, and the last three words mean 'often go awry'. Burns is addressing a mouse (the way you do) and commiserating with him that, for all his forethought in preparing a winter shelter for himself, the plough has come along and destroyed it. 'Don't beat yourself up, Mousie,' Burns says (only he says it in Scots), 'it could happen to anyone.'[33] It's a poetic way of rendering Murphy's (or Sod's) Law, which states that if something can go wrong it will. Which is, of course, so true.

33 He tactfully doesn't mention the grasshopper that is now living on welfare (*see* 'You've made your bed, so you must lie in it').

John Steinbeck's *Of Mice and Men* is a fine example of the best laid plans – sensible George trying to protect intellectually challenged Lennie from the traumas of the real world – going completely belly up. If you don't know it, rent the John Malkovich version on DVD and buy a *big* box of Kleenex on the way home.

Seeing *is believing*

THE APOSTLE WHO has come down to posterity as Doubting Thomas refused to believe that the crucified Christ had risen from the dead until he had (don't read this if you are having your lunch) put his fingers into the print of the nails in Christ's hands. Christ said, 'Because thou hast seen me, thou hast believed; blessed are they that have not seen, and yet have believed.'

Believing the evidence of your own eyes has always been popular among those who don't believe in God, and despised by those who do. Doubting Thomas should perhaps have modelled himself on Lewis Carroll's White Queen, who often believed as many as six impossible things before breakfast. Oh no, silly me, he couldn't have done. *Through the Looking-Glass* wasn't written for another 1900 years. Pity – it might have saved Thomas's reputation.

The Italians have a variation of this proverb, 'The saint has no believers unless he works miracles', and certainly very

155

few people would bother to make the trek to Lourdes (it's a real slog from a gîte in the Dordogne) if Saint Bernadette stopped doing her stuff.

Silence *is golden* …

… BUT MY eyes still see, as the 1960s hit song had it. That was sung by a guy who could see that another guy was two-timing a girl that he (the first guy) cared about, but didn't want to tell her because: 1) she would be hurt; and 2) she wouldn't believe him, even though he would continue to see what was going on. So keeping quiet wasn't so great for him. No matter, the Tremeloes got to Number One with it, so why should they care?

But keeping quiet until you know what you are talking about (*see* 'Fools rush in where angels fear to tread') has long been considered a prudent course of action. Abraham Lincoln perhaps summed it up best when he said, 'Better to remain silent and be thought a fool than to speak out and remove all doubt.'

You can't make a **silk** purse out of a sow's ear

OH FOR HEAVEN'S sake. Of course you can't. A sow's ear is not made of silk, it's made of cartilage – and hairy cartilage at that. So you couldn't make a silk *ear* out of a sow's ear, never mind a silk anything else.

In the nineteenth century, people also said, 'You cannot make a horn of a pig's tail', and in both instances it was because of some vague physical resemblance between the two objects (I suppose a curly pig's tail does look a *little* like a curly French horn. When it comes to silk purses and sows' ears, I'm sticking to my guns). The original Latin proverb, figuratively speaking, means that you can't make something good out of inferior raw materials. If you want a silk purse, just buy one next time you are in Liberty's.

Let **sleeping** dogs lie

OR *N'ESVEILLEZ PAS lou chien qui dort*, as they liked to assert in fourteenth-century France. In 1385, Chaucer expressed it thus, in *Troilus and Criseyde*: 'It is nought good a sleeping hound to wake.'

This is another of the 'It's no use crying over spilt milk'/'Least said, soonest mended' school, which also includes 'Never trouble trouble till trouble troubles you' or the simpler 'Leave well enough alone'. If you wake sleeping dogs they are likely to bark or bite, is the implication.

Of course, you can be unlucky: even a sleeping dog can cause trouble. In the Sherlock Holmes story about the racehorse Silver Blaze, it was the 'curious incident of the dog in the night-time' – the fact that the dog did nothing – that gave the game away.

There's many a **slip** 'twixt the cup and the lip

PARTICULARLY IF YOU are wearing a white top and drinking red wine, in my experience. But in a proverbial context, this is just another way of saying that you shouldn't count your chickens before they are hatched. The concept was not unknown in the ancient world, as we know from a remark by the Roman statesman Cato the Elder: *Saepe audivi inter os atque offam multa intervenire posse*, which in plain English means 'I have often heard that many things can come between mouth and morsel'.

Slow *but steady wins the race*

THIS IS THE moral of Aesop's fable about the hare and the tortoise, in which the hare brags to all the animals about how fast he is and challenges anyone who dares to race against him. The tortoise takes him on and the hare, well, hares off. However, so contemptuous is he of the tortoise's slow pace that he lies down to have a nap and wakes to find that the tortoise, who has just plodded steadily along, has beaten him to the finishing line. So think carefully before shooting your mouth off and don't take unscheduled naps on the job are the other parts of Aesop's message.

Over on the other side of the world, at very nearly the same time, Confucius was writing, 'It does not matter how slowly you go, so long as you do not stop.' It seems immensely unlikely that Confucius had read Aesop, or vice versa, so the two of them must spontaneously have had the same bright idea.

There's no **smoke** *without fire*

LATE THIRTEENTH CENTURY in origin, this means that every slanderous or libellous statement has some foundation. A faintly pernicious proverb, in my view: it's what people say, or think, when they have read bitchy gossip in the tabloids and failed to notice the retraction printed in tiny type on page 23 a few days later. It's very easy to forget, after seeing the banner headlines, that somebody subsequently won a libel case or was acquitted on a charge of shoplifting: the mud has stuck, the dog might as well be hanged.

The American journalist P. J. O'Rourke is less sympathetic to those in the public eye: 'You can't shame or humiliate modern celebrities,' he once wrote.[34] 'What used to be called shame and humiliation is now called publicity. And forget traditional character assassination. If you say a modern celebrity is an adulterer, a pervert and a drug addict, all it means is that you've read his autobiography.' The particularly interesting thing about this observation is that it was made in the very early 1990s, before celebrity culture infiltrated so many parts of our lives.

---

34 In his book *Give War a Chance: Eyewitness Accounts of Mankind's Struggle Against Tyranny, Injustice & Alcohol-Free Beer*. This man can really do subtitles: his previous works include *Driving Like Crazy: Thirty Years of Vehicular Hell-Bending, Celebrating America the Way It's Supposed to Be – With an Oil Well in Every Backyard, a Cadillac Escalade in Every Carport and the Chairman of the Federal Reserve Mowing Our Lawn*.

In addition to his masterly subtitles, the wonderful thing about P. J. O'Rourke is his scattergun approach to vitriol. Since writing the above, I have tracked down the book and find that he was considering people and things that should be 'tarred and feathered and run out of town on a rail' for pure silliness. His list includes such wide-ranging candidates as Yoko Ono, Dr Benjamin Spock, Ben and Jerry's ice cream and the TV series *M★A★S★H*. A review quoted on the back cover suggests that this 'may be the first book that would irritate both Salman Rushdie and the Ayatollah Khomeini'. Way to go, P. J.

As you **sow***, so shall you reap*

THIS IS BASED on Saint Paul writing to the Galatians: 'Whatsoever a man soweth, that shall he also reap. For he that soweth to his flesh shall of the flesh reap corruption: but he that soweth to the Spirit shall of the Spirit reap life everlasting.'

In the modern, secular sense this means you must take responsibility for your own actions (*see* 'You've made your bed, so you must lie in it') and the best (albeit misspelled) example comes from the tale of Horatio Bottomley MP, who was imprisoned in the 1920s for fraud on a spectacular scale. A prison visitor, finding him sewing mail bags, said, 'Ah, Bottomley. Sewing?'

'No,' Horatio replied. 'Reaping.'

Spare *the rod and spoil the child*

THE OLD TESTAMENT book of Proverbs, attributed in part to King Solomon, is full of variations on this theme: 'He that spareth his rod hateth his son: but he that loveth him chasteneth him betimes'; 'Foolishness is bound in the heart of a child; but the rod of correction shall drive it far from him'; 'Withhold not correction from the child: for if thou beatest him with the rod, he shall not die. Thou shalt beat him with the rod, and shalt deliver his soul from hell.' And there are plenty more where those came from.

Gosh. Solomon must have had strong views on parenting, which is odd, because his own son, Rehoboam, turned out to be a bit of a liability: on ascending the throne he promised the people that while his father had chastised them with whips, he would chastise them with scorpions. They understandably took offence, rebelled and split the Kingdom of Israel in two, leaving Rehoboam to rule over only a tiny part of it and have nothing more to leave to posterity than an outsized bottle of wine named after him.

Most people nowadays would disapprove of using a rod on children, even if it was to deliver their souls from hell, though a New Testament passage (Hebrews, chapter 12) about loving fathers chastising their sons is sometimes used as a counter-argument.[35] In the UK, corporal punishment – 'any intentional application of force for the purpose of punishment' – is illegal in schools, and human rights groups are campaigning to make hitting a child illegal under any circumstances. So it may be best to stash the rod – and the scorpions – up in the attic out of temptation's way.

---

35 The counter-counter-argument points out that this passage doesn't specify that the chastising is done with a rod.

Sticks *and stones may break my bones, but words (or names) will never hurt me*

OH, THIS ONE is so not true. Words can be really really hurtful (ask any author or actor who has ever had a bad review); as for the stick or stone, it would have to be a pretty large one to break any bones – or even break the skin. The proverb could usefully be rephrased as 'words *should* never hurt me', as a warning against the sort of paranoid hypersensitivity suffered by most authors and actors.

Still *waters run deep*

'DO NOT UNDERESTIMATE the determination of a quiet man,' said Conservative leader Iain Duncan Smith, in 2002, just a year before he lost a vote of no confidence and resigned. Said to be a Bactrian saying (from the place in Afghanistan, not the camel – so far as I know), this proverb encapsulates what he meant: it is easy to overlook someone who isn't obsessed with the sound of his (or her) own voice. When a former quietly spoken Conservative Prime Minister was revealed to have had a long affair with a colleague, the reaction was much the same: 'Who'd have thought it?' we all said. 'He wasn't so grey after all.'

A wonderful Afrikaans saying offers a more picturesque

image: *Stille waters, diepe grond, onder draai die duiwel rond*. This literally translates as 'Still waters, deep ground, underneath the devil turns round and round'. Not elegant, but you get the picture. It's the watery equivalent of 'Don't judge a book by its cover.'

In other words, the stillness of the surface, or the plainness of the cover, or the mildness of the manner, can conceal unsuspected strength, hidden passions or downright duplicity. Beware.

A **stitch** in time saves nine

THIS DATES BACK to the far-off days when you mended clothes that were torn rather than just throwing them out. In other words, fix it (whatever 'it' may be – a woollen sweater, an outbreak of ground elder in the garden, a cavity in your teeth) now, before it gets worse. If you've got to this stage you're a bit late for 'Prevention is better than cure', but better late than never. The saying seems to have been first recorded in 1732 by Thomas Fuller in his *Gnomologia, Adagies and Proverbs, Wise Sentences and Witty Sayings, Ancient and Modern, Foreign and British*, a subtitle to give P. J. O'Rourke pause (*see* There's no smoke without fire). However, Fuller's version was the slightly less confident 'A Stitch in Time *may* save nine' (italics mine).

Strike *while the iron is hot*

THIS PROVERB ALLUDES to the art of the blacksmith and not to the widely loathed modern domestic chore. Chaucer (again) in the *Tale of Melibee*, from 1386: 'While that iron is hot, men should smite.' If you were a blacksmith you would understand immediately; having heated your slab of iron until it is nice and soft and workable, you must hit it at once with your hammer to change its shape – if you wait until the metal cools again, you will have lost your chance. In other words, seize an opportunity when it presents itself, or it may be too late.

If at first you don't **succeed***, try, try again*

MALCOLM GLADWELL'S RESEARCH, quoted under 'Jack of all trades is master of none' (*see* page 111), certainly bears out the importance of perseverance as a means to achieving your ends. On the other hand, there's a smugness about this proverb that makes me prefer the advice of the actor W. C. Fields: 'If at first you don't succeed, try, try again. Then quit. No use being a damn fool about it.'

There are many finely honed pieces of cynicism attributed to W. C. Fields, notably 'Anyone who hates children and animals can't be all bad' and 'Never give a sucker an even break', but honourable mention should also be given to 'Hell, I never vote *for* anybody. I always vote *against*'.

You must **suffer** to be beautiful

THIS ASSUMES THREE things:

1.   That you aren't beautiful already

2.   That you would like to be and

3.   That the beauty you want is the skin-deep kind that can be achieved only through nip-and-tuck surgery, botox injections, starvation diets or painful treatments involving hot wax.

If that is all too much, you may find the thought that 'Handsome is as handsome does' (*see* page 99) more heartening.

One **swallow** doesn't make a summer

IN SOUTHERN EUROPE they say that one swallow doesn't make a spring, and given the difference in climate between them and the UK, both sayings are probably as true as each other. We're talking about the bird, by the way, not the first sip of Pimm's, and the point is that just because one swallow has come back from whatever sunny part of Africa it has wintered in, you shouldn't put your warm clothes into mothballs and wander round in T-shirt and shorts. More importantly, perhaps (because you can always get the warm clothes out again), it means that just because one small thing has happened (the price of property hasn't actually *fallen* this week), big things don't necessarily follow (we are coming out of a recession).

In other words, the saying – originally from Ancient Greece – is a warning against over-optimism.. If you are of a more positive frame of mind, you might prefer to quote the poet Shelley (not normally a barrel of laughs, but he scores with this one) who came up with the cheery thought that 'if Winter comes, can Spring be far behind?' So, if even a single swallow comes, his mates (or warm weather, or economic recovery) may well be on their way.

You can't **take** it with you

MEANING 'THERE IS no point in hoarding your money; it will be no use to you when you're dead.' Sometimes more picturesquely expressed as 'There are no pockets in shrouds.' While the latter is undeniable, no one has (to my knowledge) yet come back to confirm the truth of the former. Saint Paul's words to Timothy, now used in the Church of England funeral service, affirm that we brought nothing into this world and can carry nothing out of it; on the other hand, anyone who has seen the treasures harvested from the Pyramids will know that wealthy Ancient Egyptians took no chances – the Pharaohs were buried along with jewellery, furniture and servants, obviously expecting the Afterlife to fall short of the exalted standards they were used to on earth.

It's a tricky one, this: what a fool you'd feel if you'd saved all your money and then found there was nothing to spend it on in Heaven. Or indeed Hell – but my guess is that the minibars in Hell are going to be ludicrously overpriced, so it might be worth hanging on to a few quid just in case.

Talk/speak of the devil and he will appear

YOU HAVE TO believe in the devil for this saying – first recored in Torriano's *Italian Proverbs* in 1666 – to have any validity, but in the old days, when people did believe in him, they were superstitious about mentioning his name – a tradition that has persisted into modern times with You-know-who in the Harry Potter novels. An older version of the proverb is a little more scary: 'Talk of the Devil and he'll put out his horns', or in other words, reveal who he really is. Nowadays, 'Talk of the devil' means nothing more than, 'Oh hello, we were just talking about you'.

You can't **teach** an old dog new tricks

USED BY THE ageing as an excuse for not trying something new, or by the young in disparagement of their elders' abilities, this phrase dates back to the sixteenth century. The title of the TV series *New Tricks*, about three detectives dragged out of retirement to investigate old unsolved cases, may reinforce either of these interpretations. Or it may be postmodern irony, who can tell?

There's a **time** and a place for everything

THIS IS A reference to the Old Testament book of Ecclesiastes: 'To everything there is a season, and a time to every purpose under the heaven: a time to be born, and a time to die; a time to plant, and a time to pluck up that which is planted' and so forth – a time for killing, healing, keeping, losing and throwing away, loving, hating, embracing and refraining from embracing. So yes, a time for pretty much everything.[36]

This passage is often read at funerals to remind us that death is one of those things there is a time for. As such, it's of much more value than the rather priggish 'A place

36 If you're more familiar with Sixties pop than with the book of Ecclesiastes, you'll know that this was also turned into a pop song, by The Byrds in 1965.

for everything and everything in its place', which means nothing more nor less than 'How many times do I have to ask you to clean up that mess?'

Time *flies when you're enjoying yourself*

IT CERTAINLY SEEMS to. And drags in geography lessons or when you're waiting for the results of the Eurovision Song Contest. But of course time flies anyway. The Roman poet Virgil was perhaps the first to remark on 'irretrievable time' flying (that's where the Latin version, *Tempus fugit*, comes from); Chaucer and any number of more recent authors have said much the same thing, to warn us that we'll be old before we know it and won't have achieved anything. Omar Khayyám's version goes:

One thing at least is certain – This Life flies…
The flower that once is blown for ever dies

and in the seventeenth century the poet Andrew Marvell urged his coy mistress[37] to stop being so coy with the words:

The grave's a fine and private place

37 'Mistress' had a more innocent meaning in those days: it's abundantly clear in this instance that – much to his chagrin – the poet has not yet got the lady into bed.

But none, I think, do there embrace.

Nor was the twentieth century immune: Harry S. Truman spelled it out with 'It is remarkable indeed how time flies and makes you an old man' and, as the truly gloomy poem by Robert Service puts it, 'It's later than you think'.

So grasp opportunity and make the most of it. You're a long time dead.

Time *is a great healer/* *Time heals all wounds*

DATING BACK TO Ancient Greek times, though in a slightly different form, this seems to have been a truth universally acknowledged until 1951, when the novelist Ivy Compton-Burnett wrote, 'Time has too much credit It is not a great healer. It is an indifferent and perfunctory one. Sometimes it does not heal at all. And sometimes when it seems to, no healing has been necessary.' But don't listen to her – almost no one reads her any more.

Time *is money*

BENJAMIN FRANKLIN POPULARIZED this Ancient Greek idea by making it clear to even the stupidest of us: 'He that can earn ten shillings a day and sits idle one half of that day has really thrown away five shillings.'

This assumes, of course, that you are paid by results. If you have an office job in which you are effectively paid for turning up, you don't need to give a damn.

There's no **time** like the present

NEVER PUT OFF till tomorrow what you can do today, procrastination is the thief of time … yes, yes, we know.

There's many a **true** word spoken in jest

FOR INSTANCE:

- Experience is the name everyone gives to their mistakes.

- By the time you're eighty years old you've learned everything. You only have to remember it.

- Giving up smoking is the easiest thing in the world. I know because I've done it thousands of times.

- The only safe pleasure for a parliamentarian is a bag of boiled sweets.

- Not only is there no God, but try getting a plumber on weekends.[38]

Enough said?

Truth/*fact is stranger than fiction*

BYRON WROTE IN *Don Juan* (1823), 'Truth is always strange, Stranger than fiction.' But then he hadn't read *Lord of the Rings*.

Having said that, I recently heard a story on the news about a man serving time in jail in Kentucky who spends most of his waking hours filing lawsuits. So far he has run up about 4,000, against, among others, Britney Spears, George W. Bush, Che Guevara, Nostradamus, the Garden of Eden and the Eiffel Tower. He is currently – allegedly – suing *The Guinness Book of Records* for naming him the world's most litigious man. As the radio presenter who shared this with me said, you couldn't make it up.

38 Courtesy of Oscar Wilde, George Burns, Mark Twain, Julian Critchley MP and Woody Allen respectively.

There's many a good **tune** played on an old fiddle

UNTIL RECENTLY, MOST world-renowned violinists would have endorsed this and, given the choice, played a Stradivarius, an Amati or a Guarneri. But it is no longer as simple as that: almost all the surviving Cremona violins were extensively restored and modernized in the nineteenth century, which altered their tone; latterly, baroque groups trying to create an authentic sound have had their instruments unmodernized again. In the meantime, scientists are studying such things as the size of the 'f' holes and the transverse vibrations of the strings to see how exactly a violin works and whether a modern instrument-maker can create a replica Stradivarius that is more authentic than an existing Stradivarius that hasn't been unmodernized, if you see what I mean. So, give them time – it may be that good tunes will soon be able to be played on new fiddles too.

Of course this has nothing to do with the proverbial meaning, which tends to refer to the enduring sexual prowess of the older man. In this context, the hilarious dirty-old-man's song 'It's Never Too Late to Fall in Love', from *The Boyfriend* by Sandy Wilson, points out that autumn is just as nice as spring, that you can't beat an old master and that 'experience counts a lot, you know'. If you are an older man, you will doubtless have a view on this.

United *we stand, divided we fall*

THERE ARE LOTS of variations on this theme: 'Unity is strength', 'Divide and conquer', 'A house divided against itself cannot stand'. The original was used by the American republican (by which I mean 'fighter for American independence', not 'one of George Bush's supporters') Patrick Henry to denounce the increasing autonomy of the individual, newly created states of America. 'A house divided against itself' was a favourite of Abraham Lincoln's – he seems to have said it at every opportunity in the couple of years running up to his becoming president. But presumably in those pre-television days he was wandering round the country saying it to different people, so they didn't get too fed up to elect him.

The origin of the proverb is yet another of Aesop's fables, this time about a man whose sons were always quarrelling amongst themselves. The father made the sons bring him a bundle of sticks and demonstrated that it was impossible to break the whole bunch, but that each one separately was very fragile. As with sticks, so with life, was the father's point.

If all this is a bit heavy for you, you may care to know that *United We Stand* is the title of a fan magazine of Manchester United football club; if you aren't a Man U fan, it is also the name of a song that was a hit for Brotherhood of

Man in 1970. A series of flops followed and the group disbanded.[39] There's an irony in there somewhere.

Variety *is the spice of life*

Variety's the very spice of life
That gives it all its flavour.

THIS A QUOTE from an eighteenth-century poem called *The Task* (already mentioned under 'Necessity is the mother of invention'). It was written by William Cowper in response to his friend Lady Austen's request for a poem in blank verse on the subject of a sofa. Now there's a woman who should have got out more.

The poem was phenomenally popular in its day (which is bizarre, as it was written three years before King George III went mad for the first time and four years before the French Revolution – you would think that people had other things to think about). Anyway, it soon branches out from its rather niche theme to become a reflection on contemporary English life, and 'Variety's the very spice of life' is from a section dealing with the ludicrous emphasis we put on fashion; the poem goes on to say that we spend a fortune on new clothes when our old ones are hardly

---

39 Brotherhood of Man went on to win the Eurovision Song Contest in 1974 with 'Save Your Kisses for Me', as I'm sure you know, but with a completely different line-up.

worn and are quite happy to starve if our finances don't run to both finery *and* food.

As a young man Cowper had lived and worked in London, but suffered from depression and by the time he wrote *The Task* was living quietly in the country. Much of the poem compares the bustle of town unfavourably with the simple life of the country, so it is ironic that its most famous line, intended ironically, should be so often used to mean the opposite of what its author intended – having read it out of context, I had always assumed that it was referring to sex. If only he had said, 'Variety's the very spice of life – *but this is a bad thing*', we've have had a better idea what he was on about.

Virtue *is its own reward*

WELL, IT IS if you are a nice person. Some of us aren't as noble as Spiderman (*see* 'Noblesse oblige') and prefer to be paid. Or praised. Whichever. It's the recognition that matters. So what was Ovid on about when he coined the phrase: *Virtuum pretium ... esse sui*?

Walls *have ears*

NO THEY DON'T. Not usually.

The one in *Pyramus and Thisbe*, the play-within-a-play in *A Midsummer Night's Dream*, must have ears, though. Pyramus and Thisbe are in love but forbidden to meet, so they converse through a chink in the wall that separates their fathers' properties. At one point Pyramus addresses the wall with the words:

Thou wall, O wall, O sweet and lovely wall,
Show me thy chink, to blink through with mine eyne.[40]

The wall does so and Pyramus thanks it, so it seems safe to assume that it has heard the request. When Pyramus and Thisbe have finished their conversation, the wall utters its only lines, to the effect that it has served its purpose so it's going away now, suggesting that it was a mouth as well. But as this wall is played by Snout the Tinker, not made of bricks and mortar, it may be yet another exception that proves the rule.

All this is, of course, ignoring the underlying meaning of the proverb, which is, 'Be careful what you say. You never know who might be listening' (*see* 'Little pitchers have big ears').

---

40 *Pyramus and Thisbe* is a melodramatic parody, so if your reaction to these lines is that they are not the acme of Shakespeare's poetic achievement, you are showing the sort of critical judgement of which Alexander Pope would have been proud (*see* 'Fools rush in where angels fear to tread').

A **watched** pot never boils

CLEARLY NONSENSE, SAY the 'never say never' brigade. As long as you put heat under it, it is bound to boil sooner or later. There's probably a law of thermodynamics about it. What it means, of course, is that something that you are eagerly anticipating (like a cup of tea, presumably) seems to take longer to arrive if you sit around waiting for it. An earlier variation was 'A watched pot is long in boiling', which makes more sense but doesn't sound as good. There are a lot of these triumphs of style over substance in the proverb world (*see*, for example, *Plus ça change, plus c'est la même chose* and 'It never rains but it pours').

Where there's a **will** there's a way

DATING BACK TO the mid-seventeenth century, this means 'You can do anything if you want to hard enough.' Probably not strictly true – I am never going to play for England (at anything) – but a useful one for keeping the spirits up when the going gets tough. But remember also the cautionary words of W. C. Fields under 'If at first you don't succeed...'.

Even a **worm** will turn

THE WELSH SAY, 'It's the quiet dog that bites' and this is not a million miles from 'Still waters run deep' (*see* page 164) – in the one case, there may be hidden passion behind a quiet exterior; in the other, you can push even the mildest person only so far before they suddenly decide that they have had enough. You may then find that you have opened a can of worms and would have been better to let sleeping dogs lie.

Two **wrongs** don't make a right

DATING BACK TO the late 1700s, this is very true, but if you are feeling vindictive you might like to give thought to the idea that 'Revenge is a dish best served cold' (*see* page 149).

You're only **young** once

See 'Boys will be boys', page 44.

Zeal *without knowledge is the sister of folly*

NO, I'D NEVER heard this either, but it seemed feeble to end the book with the '*see* page 44' above. Once I started searching for 'z's I found several variations on this theme, including 'Zeal without knowledge is fire without light' and 'Zeal without prudence is frenzy.' The 'sister of folly' version is a quote from a book called *The Scourge of Folly* by John Davies of Hereford, a contemporary of Shakespeare.

A nineteenth-century American called Levi Carroll Judson obviously felt even more strongly on the subject: he wrote in a book with the not desperately sexy title of *The Moral Probe: Or One Hundred and Two Common Sense Essays on the Nature of Men and Things*, 'Zeal, without knowledge, is slavery in its highest refinement. It blinds its subjects, and renders them the dupes of knaves.'

In other words, rushing in where angels fear to tread is not just foolish – according to Levi it is positively dangerous. So zeal is dangerous, a little learning is dangerous, all work and no play is dangerous, giving a dog a bad name is dangerous, putting all your eggs in one basket is dangerous, giving a man enough rope is potentially fatal – I'm beginning to wish I hadn't started this. Shall we go back to 'All's well that ends well' and leave it at that?

Bibliography

Brewer's Dictionary of Phrase and Fable (14th edition, Cassell, 1989)

George B. Bryan & Wolfgang Mieder, *A Dictionary of Anglo-American Proverbs and Proverbial Phrases* (Peter Lang, 2005)

Harry Collis, *101 American English Proverbs* (McGraw Hill, 1992)

Linda & Roger Flavell, *Dictionary of Proverbs and their Origins* (revised edition, Kyle Cathie, 2004)

Malcolm Gladwell, *Outliers: The Story of Success* (Allen Lane, 2008)

Colin Gough, 'Science and the Stradivarius' in *Physics World* (2000)

Sir Paul Harvey, *The Oxford Companion to English Literature* (4th edition, Oxford University Press, 1967)

Sir Paul Harvey & J. E. Heseltine, *The Oxford Companion to French Literature* (Oxford University Press, 1959)

Elizabeth Knowles (ed.), *Oxford Dictionary of Modern Quotations* (3rd edition, Oxford University Press, 2007)

The Oxford Dictionary of Phrase, Saying and Quotation (Oxford University Press, 1997)

Lao-Tzu, *Tao Te Ching*, trans. Stephen Mitchell (Kyle Cathie, 1996)

Bruce M. Metzger & Michael D. Coogan, *The Oxford Companion to the Bible* (Oxford University Press, 1993)

Wolfgang Mieder, *The Politics of Proverbs* (University of Wisconsin Press, 1997)

—*The Proverbial Abraham Lincoln* (Peter Lang, 2000)

P. J. O'Rourke, *Give War a Chance: Eyewitness Accounts of Mankind's Struggle Against Tyranny, Injustice & Alcohol-Free Beer* (Picador, 1992)

Matthew Parris, *Great Parliamentary Scandals* (Robson, 1996)

Angela Partington (ed.), *The Oxford Dictionary of Quotations* (revised 4th edition, 1996)

Nigel Rees, *All Gong and No Dinner* (Collins, 2007)

Jennifer Speake (ed.), *The Oxford Dictionary of Proverbs* (5th edition, Oxford University Press, 2008)

I also found lots of information about Ovid at www.sacred-texts.com and about Voltaire at www.whitman.edu/VSA/trois.imposteurs.html

Other titles in the same series, all priced £5.99:

i before e (except after c):
old-school ways to remember stuff
by Judy Parkinson

978–1–84317–658–9 in paperback format
978–1–84317–431–8 in ePub format
978–1–84317–432–5 in Mobipocket format

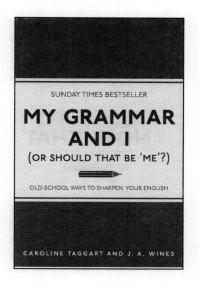

My Grammar and I (or should that be 'Me'?):
old-school ways to sharpen your English
by Caroline Taggart and J. A. Wines

978-1-84317-657-2 in paperback format
978-1-84317-626-8 in ePub format
978-1-84317-528-5 in Mobipocket format

I Used to Know That: stuff you forgot from school
by Caroline Taggart

978-1-84317-655-8 in paperback format
978-1-84317-605-3 in ePub format
978-1-84317-606-0 in Mobipocket format

I Think, Therefore I Am:
all the philosophy you need to know
by Leslie Levene

978-1-78243-024-7 in paperback format
978-1-84317-601-5 in ePub format
978-1-84317-602-2 in Mobipocket format

A Classical Education:
the stuff you wish you'd been taught at school
by Caroline Taggart

978-1-78243-010-0 in paperback format
978-1-84317-607-7 in ePub format
978-1-84317-530-8 in Mobipocket format

An Apple a Day:
old-fashioned proverbs and why they still work
by Caroline Taggart

978-1-78243-009-4 in paperback format
978-1-84317-652-7 in ePub format
978-1-84317-529-2 in Mobipocket format

I Wandered Lonely as a Cloud:
and other poems you half remember from school
by Ana Sampson

978-1-78243-012-4 in paperback format

Spilling the Beans on the Cat's Pyjamas:
popular expressions — what they mean and
where we got them

978-1-78243-011-7 in paperback format
978-1-84317-667-1 in ePub format
978-1-84317-668-8 in Mobipocket format